PENGUIN  CLASSICS

HESIOD AND THEOGNIS

ADVISORY EDITOR: BETTY RADICE

Very little is known about HESIOD and it cannot definitely be proved that the same man wrote both the *Theogony* and *Works and Days*. He probably lived in the eighth century BC (contemporary with Homer) in Boeotia on the Greek mainland.

THEOGNIS lived and wrote chiefly in the sixth century BC. He came from Megara, probably the one on the Greek mainland, and was an aristocrat. There was a popular revolution, in which he lost his status and possibly his money. He appears to have been exiled and might have moved to Megara in Sicily. He had a friend called Kurnos, the son of Polypaos, an aristocrat like himself, to whom he wrote numerous poems.

DOROTHEA SCHMIDT WENDER was born in 1934 in Ohio and graduated from Radcliffe College, and then went to the University of Minnesota and Harvard University. She is a retired Professor and Chairman of the Department of Classics at Wheaton College, Massachusetts. Her publications include three scholarly books, two murder mysteries, one juvenile novel, and many book reviews and articles in both classics and medicine.

HESIOD

THEOGONY · WORKS AND DAYS

THEOGNIS

ELEGIES

Translated and with introductions
by Dorothea Wender

PENGUIN BOOKS

PENGUIN BOOKS

Published by the Penguin Group
Penguin Books Ltd, 80 Strand, London WC2R 0RL, England
Penguin Putnam Inc., 375 Hudson Street, New York, New York 10014, USA
Penguin Books Australia Ltd, 250 Camberwell Road, Camberwell, Victoria 3124, Australia
Penguin Books Canada Ltd, 10 Alcorn Avenue, Toronto, Ontario, Canada M4V 3B2
Penguin Books India (P) Ltd, 11 Community Centre, Panchsheel Park, New Delhi – 110 017, India
Penguin Books (NZ) Ltd, Cnr Rosedale and Airborne Roads, Albany, Auckland, New Zealand
Penguin Books (South Africa) (Pty) Ltd, 24 Sturdee Avenue, Rosebank 2196, South Africa

Penguin Books Ltd, Registered Offices: 80 Strand, London WC2R 0RL, England

www.penguin.com

This translation first published 1973

050

Translation and Introduction copyright © Dorothea Wender, 1973
All rights reserved

Printed and bound in Great Britain by Clays Ltd, Elcograf S.p.A.

Set in Monotype Ehrhardt

ISBN-13: 978-0-14-044283-0

www.greenpenguin.co.uk

TO MY MOTHER

MARGARET CHASE SCHMIDT

WRITER, TEACHER, CLASSICIST

Contents

HESIOD

Introduction

THE poems of Hesiod were probably composed at about the same time as the poems of Homer, perhaps towards the end of the eighth century B.C. But while the tradition in Asia Minor, where Homer lived, produced epics designed for an upper-class audience, the tradition in Boeotia (Hesiod's district, on the Greek mainland) produced more pedestrian works: genealogies, catalogues, handbooks on divination, astronomy, ethics, farming, and metal work. These were not all produced by one man. There must have been a fair number of poets working in Boeotia at any one time; the *Works and Days* says that minstrel competes with minstrel as carpenter does with carpenter. But only three products of the Boeotian school have come down to us in anything more than fragmentary form: the *Theogony*, the *Works and Days*, and the *Shield of Heracles*. This last (largely modelled on Achilles' shield in *Iliad* 18) is a rather poor piece of work, seldom regarded as Hesiod's, and so not included in this translation. Most ancient Greeks called the author of the first two of these by the name of Hesiod. They passed on several vivid and improbable stories about him – that he beat Homer in a singing contest, that he committed adultery with a host's sister, and fathered the Locrian poet Stesichorus, that he was murdered for his crime, and that his body was thrown out to sea but brought back by dolphins.*

*The earliest reference to Hesiod's violent death is in Thucydides (3.96.1). The story, more or less embellished, is referred to several times in the Palatine Anthology (vii. 54 and 55) and more fully described by Plutarch (*Septem Sapientum Convivium*, xix. 162), Pausanias (31. 6; 38. 3), and the *Suda* (under Hesiodus). Tzetzes (*Life of Hesiod*) tells the whole lurid story, dolphins and all. References to the contest with Homer are found in Plutarch (op. cit., x. 153), Pausanias (31. 3) and *The Contest of Homer and Hesiod* (to be found in volume V of Homer's Works, Oxford Classical Texts), a

These fantasies are clearly not much help to us. Who really was Hesiod, and what do we know of him? Did he write both the *Theogony* and the *Works and Days*? Which is the earlier of the two?

I will answer the last question first, for I think it is the easiest. I believe that the *Theogony* is the earlier poem. There are many reasons for this conclusion (West and Solmsen* give a number of them), but the strongest is to be found in a comparison of line 225 of the *Theogony* with lines 11–26 of the *Works and Days*. The discussion of the two Strifes in the latter poem seems like a deliberate revision of the account of the birth of Strife in the *Theogony*.

Did the same man write both works? Modern scholarly opinion is divided on this question; two of the best recent editors of Hesiod (Solmsen and West) have argued for unity of authorship, as has the fine critic and translator Richmond Lattimore, but the weight of opinion generally has come down rather heavily on the other side. I am afraid I must agree with the majority, although with some misgivings. I began these translations with a strong prejudice in favour of one Hesiod – partly, because I am a staunch unitarian about Homer – but the longer I spent with the poems and the deeper I got into the texts, the more uneasy I became about this man Hesiod. The *Theogony* was such a strain to translate; I kept having to check an impulse to improve it a little, on nearly every page. It was wonderful, exciting material (primitive gods, big dark forces, sex, violence, world catastrophes, etc.), but the writer had managed to make so much of it tedious. The *Works and Days* was a pleasure to work on, and full of surprises. I kept discovering more in the style than I had noticed at first, and, as with Theognis, my main problem as a translator was to transfer the artistry of the original into English, not to lose the neat turn of phrase or the subtly implied metaphor. And this was the poem I had dreaded, expecting dull moralizing and a farmer's almanac.

---

document of dubious date and authorship, which also describes the death of Hesiod.

*See Bibliography, p. 22.

My reason, then, for believing Hesiod to be two men is exactly the same as my reason for thinking Homer only one: quality. This is a personal, non-quantifiable argument, which I cannot expect anyone to accept as 'evidence', although I shall try later in the introduction to point out more concretely some of the characteristics of the styles of the *Theogony* and the *Works and Days*. I do admit that it is *possible* that Hesiod might have written the *Theogony* when he was very young and still struggling with the physical problem of writing. (I believe, for reasons we haven't space for, that both works, as well as the *Iliad* and *Odyssey* in the form we have them, were written down, not orally composed.) Then, somehow, this same Hesiod might have learned – perhaps from reading Homer – how to write well enough to produce the *Works and Days*. But I can't think of another author in whom the contrast between one work and another is so great. The worst plays of Aeschylus, and of Shakespeare, are pretty tedious, but their style, line for line, is not so bad; it is the substance that fails. To be sure, a poet's style may change: Yeats is a good example, but his earlier, fancier, old-fashioned style was nevertheless good for what it was; it was just a different sort of style. Robert Burns' English poems and his Scots poems are very different, and most would agree that his Scots poems are far more effective, but even in the English poems he clearly shows that he is no amateur.

However, if the two Hesiodic works are by different authors, there is another problem, the signature passage at the beginning of the *Theogony*. The poet says 'The Muses once taught lovely song to Hesiod, when he was pasturing his lambs below holy Helicon. And the goddesses, Olympian Muses, daughters of aegis-bearing Zeus, said these words first to me: "You rustic shepherds, shame!"' There are two ways of interpreting this passage, but I think Solmsen is convincing when he argues that 'Hesiod' and 'me' are the same person.* In other words, Hesiod is the author of the *Theogony*. But Hesiod was always considered the name of the poet of the *Works and Days*, even by the ancients who believed there were two poets. Also, the author of

* *Hesiod and Aeschylus*, p. 5.

the *Works and Days* says (ll. 656–9) that he once won a tripod in a singing contest in Chalcis, and set it up for the Muses of Helicon 'in the place where they first made me embark on clear-voiced singing'. (West thinks the song for which Hesiod won the tripod was in fact the *Theogony*, and he has some attractive arguments for this view,* although it's a bit hard to believe the judges would have been willing to sit through all those generations of Nereids, Oceanids and Rivers when there were probably chariot-races on the programme, too.) These two Muse passages look like fairly convincing proof of single authorship – unless the signature passage is a forgery.

I think there is another possible explanation: that Hesiod was in fact the name of the author of the *Theogony*, as he says, and not of the author of the *Works and Days*. The *Theogony* was written first, and not only made a name for its author, but started a trend of looking for poetic inspiration on Helicon, rather than in Pieria, where the cult of the Muses originated. After all, if Hesiod, a simple shepherd, met the Muses there, they must live there. Probably all the young men who aspired to creativity and had read the *Theogony* began to frequent the place, with or without lambs. We can even imagine the locals making rather a good thing of it, setting up signs marking the exact spot where the divine revelation was received, selling laurel branches and so forth, perhaps even offering singing lessons for a fee. And no doubt many of the young men received inspiration as advertised – including one of the local young men, not a shepherd but a farmer, from Askra, a nearby town. Although he had to support himself by farming, this young man had talent, sang a hymn at the funeral games in Chalcis and won a tripod, which he set up at the Muses' shrine, where no doubt there were other trophies already dedicated to Hesiod's Muses by other successful graduates. But this young man couldn't afford to be a professional bard, travelling to contests, because his father died, and he had some legal troubles with his brother Perses, and he owned some land. So he went back to farming, and the daily grind almost obscured his talents forever, until Perses ran

* M. L. West, ed., *Hesiod, Theogony*, pp. 42–6.

into money troubles and came back to his solid brother for a loan.

At this point the farmer (no longer a young man) had the happy idea of giving Perses something better than money – he would write him a long poem, full of advice about how to stay out of debt. The farmer didn't put his own name into the poem, but he talked about Perses, and about his father who had emigrated to Boeotia from Cyme in Aeolis, and about his tripod, and everyone in Askra knew who had written it, anyway. Perhaps he left a copy, for safekeeping, with the keepers of the Muses' shrine. After he died, the farmer's book became associated with all those other didactic works that kept pouring out of the shrine of the Muses on Helicon (sometimes called Hesiod's shrine), and like most of those works, this poem was called the work of Hesiod. Eventually, since this was much the best of those works, the farmer began to be thought of as *the* Hesiod.

This is all rather fanciful, of course, but I don't see why something like this might not have happened. But let us go on to the poems themselves.

Theogony

Although I have been and will again be rather mean about the style of the *Theogony*, I must admit that the material contained in it is fascinating. After a long introductory hymn to the Muses, the poet traces the history of the world, from primeval Chaos to the establishment of Zeus as supreme king of the gods. The chronology is as follows: first Chaos, then Gaia (Earth), Tartarus (the deepest underworld) and Eros (Love) appeared, apparently by spontaneous generation. Chaos gave birth to Erebos (another part of the underworld) and Night; Night mated with Erebos and produced Day and Space. Gaia produced Ouranos (Heaven), the hills, and the sea. She mated with her son Ouranos and bore Oceanus (the river which encircles the earth) and eleven more 'older' gods, the Titans, of whom the youngest was clever Kronos. Then she produced some monsters; Ouranos didn't like them, so he hid them inside Gaia.

This made the poor earth uncomfortable, so she plotted with her son Kronos to overthrow his father. He then castrated Ouranos with a long jagged sickle. The blood produced the Furies, the Giants and the ash-tree nymphs; the severed genitals themselves floated out to sea, and from the foam around them rose the beautiful goddess of love, Aphrodite. Meanwhile, Night was giving birth to a crowd of abstractions like Death, Sleep, Blame, Sorrow, the Fates, Nemesis (Retribution) and Strife. Many more births followed, from various parents: salt-water nymphs, monsters, rivers, fresh-water nymphs, Sun, Moon, Dawn, stars, the goddess Hecate, and so forth, and finally Kronos and the Titan Rhea produced the first generation of Olympians: Hestia, Demeter, Hera, Hades, Poseidon, and Zeus. But Kronos, wanting to rule forever, took to swallowing his children, until Rhea (with the help of her parents Ouranos and Gaia) saved the infant Zeus and gave Kronos a stone to swallow; eventually Kronos disgorged his other children as well. The Titan Iapetos produced, among others, Prometheus, the friend of man, and Epimetheus, who received Pandora, the first woman and source of evils for men. The next highlight in the story is the battle of the Titans and the Olympians for supremacy, featuring a tremendous display of thunder and lightning by Zeus. The defeated Titans were imprisoned in Tartarus, Zeus put down one more threat to his regime, the monster Typhoeus, and finally set his kingdom in order and fathered a number of useful children.

All this is clearly quite different from the graceful world of Homer's Olympian gods. The gods of the *Iliad* and *Odyssey*, although not perhaps very admirable ethically (they lie, cheat, steal, manhandle each other, play favourites and commit adultery rather more than Homer's humans do), are still fully anthropomorphic and civilized, and the poet has erased from their past every trace of castration, child-swallowing, incest, and other primitive behaviour, just as he has eliminated from his human world almost every trace of witchcraft, magic, human sacrifice, and homosexuality. Of course, Hesiod's poem doesn't deal with the Olympians primarily; his story ends with the establishment of their reign; but there is no apparent attempt to whitewash the mythological past in terms of modern standards, with one exception. The exception is Zeus, the hero of the poem, whose omniscience, power and justice are stressed at every opportunity. For example, in the Prometheus story, it is fairly clear that in the original version, Zeus was really fooled by Prometheus' trick about the sacrifice. But Hesiod felt it necessary to add that, since Zeus knows everything, he was not deceived, and deliberately allowed the gods to be cheated out of the better share, because he wanted to punish Prometheus. Also, Zeus' dethroning of Kronos is de-emphasized to the point of confusing vagueness, presumably because Hesiod did not want to have his hero too blatantly showing disrespect for a parent.

With the exception of Zeus, then, Hesiod has allowed his world of primitive gods and chaotic forces to remain primitive and chaotic. Particularly striking is the general pattern of an oedipal struggle between generations, with father attempting to destroy son, and mother assisting son to supplant father. There is some evidence (though it is not as clear or striking as some scholars assert) that much of Hesiod's material traces back ultimately to the older literature of the Middle East, particularly the Babylonian *Enuma Elish*;* but we have to remember that there are some basic motifs (e.g., castration of one's father, parent swallowing child, the earth literally giving birth, etc.) which are always appearing, independently, in the mythologies of primitive peoples and the fantasies of small children. The Incas of Peru had a story about the origin of diseases which parallels the Pandora myth more strikingly than many of the Middle Eastern myths which have been cited as obvious sources of Hesiod.† Clearly Hesiod did not invent the main features of his tale. Perhaps for personal reasons he gave the Muses and the goddess Hekate a particularly full treatment; probably he made up many of the names of Nereids and Oceanids and the evil

*See *Poems of Heaven and Hell from Ancient Mesopotamia* trans. N. K. Sandars, Penguin, 1972.

† T. A. Sinclair, *Hesiod; Works and Days*, Hildesheim, 1966, p. 13, quoting Frazer's commentary on Pausanias.

abstractions borne by Strife, but most of his story must have been derived from established tradition, whether it was originally Indo-European, Oriental or purely Greek.

The *Theogony* is an early work, as I have pointed out, and perhaps was composed by a man struggling, for the first time, with the problem of written composition; therefore it seems ungenerous to attack its poet for not having a polished style. (After all, many college students, and even some professors, write less clearly than Hesiod.) If, therefore, I do criticize, I trust the reader will understand that I do so only to deepen his appreciation of the 'other' Hesiod, the author of the *Works and Days*. What are the chief flaws in the *Theogony*, from a literary standpoint?

First, the poet's sense of proportion seems wrong: he devotes too little space to a number of inherently dramatic and interesting episodes (e.g., the dethroning of Kronos, any of the monster-slayings), and too much space to topics of limited appeal (e.g., the functions of Hekate). From a modern standpoint there are too many names, and too many births of relatively colourless deities, but no doubt the audience of Hesiod's day was more tolerant of them, considering the material religiously significant. Second, the poet is often ambiguous or unclear. For example: 'She bore Chimaera, who breathed awful fire.'* 'She' might be the Hydra, or Echidna, or even Ceto. Another example: the poet never tells us when mankind enters the picture. Third, Hesiod repeatedly spoils his dramatic effects by making his hero too invincible; as in the Prometheus episode, the Titan war, and the battle with Typhoeus. No adversary of Zeus gets in a single point; there is no suspense because there is never a conflict worth taking seriously. Homer gets more excitement out of a footrace than Hesiod does out of a full-scale war in heaven. The problem is not just in the Zeus episodes; the same thing is true of conflicts which don't include Zeus. Ouranos allows himself to be castrated without a murmur, and no monster is seen putting up a fight against his slayer. One is forced to conclude that Hesiod simply didn't know how to describe conflict in an

* *Theogony*, 319, p. 33.

exciting way. It is something to do with a limited point of view; Hesiod can see only one person on stage at a time. When he is writing about the castration of Ouranos, his mind is rigidly fixed on Kronos and his terrible act, to the complete exclusion of the victim. Not only is he unable to visualize an exciting conflict; he can't even seem to visualize a plausible one. Fourth, his use of language is not very skilful. At best, it is simple and euphonious. The catalogues have this virtue: the names of the Nereids roll along rather musically. But at worst, he is awkward and repetitious. Whether he is saying the same thing over and over in the same words, as in the hymns to the Muses and to Hecate, or in different words, as in the description of Pandora ('From her is the race of female women, from her is the deadly race and tribe of ladies' *), he seems to be at his worst when he is trying to do his best. When he wants to build a big climax, he almost invariably overdoes it, as in the battle with the Titans, where he keeps saying thunder!, lightning!, fire!, flame!, lightning!, thunderbolt!, crash!, blaze!, until the reader becomes quite jaded and unshakeable.

It is not all quite so dismal as I have made it out, of course. And the *Theogony* has an undoubted historical interest. But if the reader wants to find the work of a real poet, he should turn to the *Works and Days*.

Works and Days

This poem, a mixture of mythology, ethical maxims, a farmer's calendar, some tips on sailing and a collection of wise and superstitious sayings, is really one long hymn to work and prudence. In it, the poet tells his no-good brother Perses just about everything he has learned about life, in his presumably long and hard career scratching a living from the soil in miserable Askra. Hesiod (I shall call him that, for convenience) is a remarkably consistent man, and a strong, lifelike picture of his personality emerges from the poem. He is a grouchy old farmer; he mistrusts 'lords' but has no ideas about changing society. He believes in

Theogony, 590, p. 42.

justice, honesty, conventional piety, self-reliance, self-denial, foresight, and *work*. He dislikes city folk, the sea, women, gossip and *laziness*. He delivers a maxim like 'Don't urinate where the Sun can see you' with the same earnest conviction that he advises judges not to take bribes, his brother to avoid pride, and the farmer to get two nine-year-old oxen and a forty-year-old hired man. He is sometimes so serious about trivia as to make the modern reader smile, and much of the material in the poem is of purely historical interest, or is amusing because it is quaint and naive. Many of us find his conservatism, pessimism, didacticism, misogyny and lack of fun quite uncongenial. But he deserves respect, nonetheless; in the first place, because his advice to Perses was sincere, serious, and quite probably correct. If Perses had followed Hesiod's advice to the letter (although it's hard to imagine that he ever did), he *would* most probably have got out of debt and regained his self-respect. The poet's ethical advice is narrow, joyless and old-fashioned, but there is nothing laughable about it; it is a remarkably consistent and well-articulated prescription for how to be a well-adjusted and successful peasant. In the second place, Hesiod deserves our respect because he is a good poet.

The author of the *Theogony* often fails because he overdoes things: he uses too many words, too many strong adjectives where weak ones would do, too much heavy artillery when he wants to swat a fly. This is precisely what the poet of the *Works and Days* does not do. His tone is almost always restrained and appropriate, and when he wants to make a point he knows how to build a climax and speak strongly; he has not used up all his ammunition on trivia. Read, for example, his description of the fifth age of man, the iron age. He makes point after point about man's degeneracy, piling one on another with cumulative heaviness, until he reaches his smashing conclusion:

> and everywhere
> Harsh-voiced and sullen-faced and loving harm,
> Envy will walk along with wretched men.
> Last to Olympus from the broadpathed Earth
> Hiding their loveliness in robes of white

To join the gods, abandoning mankind
Will go the spirits Righteousness and Shame.
And only grievous troubles will be left
For men, and no defence against our wrongs.*

He also understands, as the poet of the *Theogony* does not,
how to use contrast to heighten an effect, and how to shift
quickly from one image to another, in order to manipulate his
reader's reactions to make an emotional point. In the poem on
winter, for example (pp. 75-7), he begins by describing the
effect of Boreas, the North Wind, on the inanimate world, the
pastures of Thrace, the sea, the forest, and the individual trees
of the forest. Then he moves to the animate: 'The animals
shudder, with tails between their legs; they find no help in furry
hides, the cold goes through even the shaggy-breasted.' Now
he moves on to man: 'He makes the old man bend, round-
shouldered as a wheel.' Now, a contrast:

He does not pierce the soft-skinned girl who stays
Indoors at home, with mother, innocent
Of golden Aphrodite's works. She bathes
Her tender skin, anoints herself with oil,
And going to an inner room at home,
She takes a nap upon a winter day.†

Isn't that a wonderful picture? The soft, clean, rich virgin, in a
house so grand and warm she can take baths in the winter, a girl
so free from all the usual cares of men (unpierced by Boreas,
innocent also of sex and work) that she takes a nap in the after-
noon. By contrast, she makes the poor round-shouldered old
man seem even more pitiful, and makes the envious reader
shiver all the more.

It should be clear from this passage that here is a poet in
control of his material, who knows how to select and arrange
his images for effect, and who knows enough not to say too
much.

If the same man who listed the powers of Hekate in the

*Works and Days, 195 ff., p. 65.
† Works and Days, 519, ff., p. 75.

Theogony also described the effects of Boreas in the *Works and Days*, then I certainly would conclude that the Muses did not limit their instruction of Hesiod to that first encounter on Helicon.

The metre of both the *Theogony* and the *Works and Days* is dactylic hexameter, the metre of Homer and of most long works in Greek and Latin. I have done my translation in blank verse (unrhymed iambic pentameter) because I think that, in feeling, it is the closest English equivalent. I have not used prose or very colloquial English because the language in both poems is rather old-fashioned and distinctly 'literary'; a mixture of dialects is used; and it is not at all the way people normally spoke in Hesiod's day.

Bibliography

My translation of the *Theogony* is based on the Greek text of M. L. West (Oxford University Press, 1966), compared with those of H. G. Evelyn-White (Loeb Library, 1968) and Friedrich Solmsen (Oxford Classical Text, 1970). For the *Works and Days* I used Evelyn-White, Solmsen, and T. A. Sinclair (Hildesheim, 1966).

There is a good deal of literature on Hesiod. I would suggest that the interested reader consult West's long and excellent introduction, Solmsen's *Hesiod and Aeschylus* (Cornell, 1949), P. Walcot's *Hesiod and the Near East* (Cardiff, 1966), Sinclair's introduction, and if he can find a copy, J. Mair's *Hesiod* (Oxford, 1908), which has wonderful appendices on Hesiod's agriculture and astronomy. Other translations (with interesting prefaces) are Richmond Lattimore's (Ann Arbor, 1959) and Norman O. Brown's (Library of Liberal Arts, 1953).

Hesiod, *Theogony*

[handwritten: daughters of zeus + memory?]

WITH the Heliconian Muses let us start
Our song: they hold the great and godly mount
Of Helicon, and on their delicate feet *[handwritten: gods can]*
They dance around the darkly bubbling spring
And round the altar of the mighty Zeus.
[handwritten: physical entities] They wash their soft skin in the Horses' Spring
Or in Permessus or Olmeius, then
Dance, fair and graceful, on the mountain-top
And whirl their feet about. Then they rise up
Wrapped in a mist, and go at night, to hymn
With lovely voices, aegis-bearing Zeus,
And lady Hera of Argos, she who goes
On golden sandals, and the maid, grey-eyed
Athene, daughter of aegis-bearing Zeus;
Phoebus Apollo, Artemis, who delights
In arrows, and Poseidon, he who shakes
The earth and holds it, Themis, much revered,
And Aphrodite, flirting with her eyes,
Golden-crowned Hebe, fair Dione, then
Leto and crooked Kronos, Iapetos,
Eos, great Helios, bright Selene,
Gaia and mighty Ocean, and at last
Black Night and all the other immortal gods
Who live forever, all that holy race.

[handwritten: methaphor for a pleasing song]
The Muses once taught Hesiod to sing
Sweet songs, while he was shepherding his lambs
On holy Helicon; the goddesses
Olympian, daughters of Zeus who holds
The aegis, first addressed these words to me:

23

'You rustic shepherds, shame: bellies you are,
Not men! We know enough to make up lies
Which are convincing, but we also have
The skill, when we've a mind, to speak the truth.'

So spoke the fresh-voiced daughters of great Zeus
And plucked and gave a staff to me, a shoot
Of blooming laurel, wonderful to see,
And breathed a sacred voice into my mouth
With which to celebrate the things to come
And things which were before. They ordered me
To sing the race of blessed ones who live
Forever, and to hymn the Muses first
And at the end. No more delays; begin:[1]

We start then, with the Muses, who delight
With song the mighty mind of father Zeus
Within Olympus, telling of things that are,
That will be, and that were, with voices joined
In harmony.[2] The sweet sound flows from mouths
That never tire; the halls of father Zeus
The Thunderer, shine gladly when the pure
Voice of the goddesses is scattered forth;
The echo spreads to snowy Olympus' peak
And the immortals' homes. Then sending out
Unearthly music, first they celebrate
The august race of first-born gods, whom Earth
Bore to broad Heaven, then their progeny,
Givers of good things. Next they sing of Zeus
The father of gods and men, how high he is
Above the other gods, how great in strength.
Next the Olympian Muses, daughters of Zeus
Who holds the aegis, sing the mighty race
Of Giants, and they please the mind of Zeus.
The goddess who protects Eleuther's hills,
Memory, bore them in Pieria
To the father, son of Kronos, and they bring
Forgetfulness of evil, rest from pain.

24

Far from the other gods, counsellor Zeus
Entered her holy bed and lay with her
Nine nights. And when the proper time arrived,
The months declined, and the seasons came around
And many days were finished, she gave birth
On snowy Olympus, not far from the peak,
To nine like-minded daughters, whose one thought
Is singing, and whose hearts are free from care.
There on Olympus are their lovely homes,
Their polished dancing-floors. And next to them
Desire and the Graces have their homes
And live in happiness. With their sweet voice
They praise the laws and courteous ways of all
The immortals, uttering their lovely sounds.[3]
They went, once, to Olympus, revelling
In their sweet voice, their heavenly song; black earth
Echoed around the singers; lovely noise
Rose from beneath their feet as they went up
To their father. He had become the king in heaven
And held the thunder and bright lightning-shaft,
For he had beaten his father, Kronos, by force,
And now divided power among the gods
Fairly, and gave appropriate rank to each.

So sang the Muses of Olympus, nine
Daughters begotten by almighty Zeus,
Cleio, Euterpe, and Melpomene,
Thalia, Erato and Terpsichore,
Polymnia, Urania, and most
Important one of all, Calliope,
For she attends upon respected lords.[4]
And when the daughters of great Zeus would bring
Honour upon a heaven-favoured lord
And when they watch him being born, they pour
Sweet dew upon his tongue, and from his lips
Flow honeyed words. All people look to him
When he is giving judgement uprightly,

25

And speaking with assurance, he can stop
Great quarrels sensibly. Wise lords are wise
In this: when public harm is being done
To the people, they can set things straight with ease,
Advising with soft words. And when a lord
Comes into the assembly, he is wooed
With honeyed reverence, just like a god,
And is conspicuous above the crowd,
Such is the Muses' holy gift to men.   *Giving lords honey words*

The Muses and Apollo, he who shoots
From far away, bring minstrels to the earth,   *→ entertainer*
And players on the lyre; lords are from Zeus.
And he is lucky whom the Muses love.
His voice flows sweetly from his mouth, and when
A man has sorrow newly on his mind
And grieves until his heart is parched within,
If a bard, the servant of the Muses, sings
The glorious deeds the men of old performed,
And hymns the blessed ones, Olympian gods,
At once that man forgets his heavy heart,
And has no memory of any grief,
So quick the Muses' gift diverts his mind.   *forgetful of grief*

Hail, daughters of Zeus! Give me sweet song,
To celebrate the holy race of gods
Who live forever, sons of starry Heaven
And Earth, and gloomy Night, and salty Sea.
Tell how the gods and earth arose at first,
And rivers and the boundless swollen sea
And shining stars, and the broad heaven above,
And how the gods divided up their wealth
And how they shared their honours, how they first
Captured Olympus with its many folds.
Tell me these things, Olympian Muses, tell
From the beginning, which first came to be?

creation account

Chaos was first of all, but next appeared
Broad-bosomed Earth, sure standing-place for all
The gods who live on snowy Olympus' peak,
And misty Tartarus, in a recess
Of broad-pathed earth, and Love, most beautiful
Of all the deathless gods. He makes men weak,
He overpowers the clever mind, and tames
The spirit in the breasts of men and gods.
From Chaos came black Night and Erebos. = *darkness*
And Night in turn gave birth to Day and Space⁵
Whom she conceived in love to Erebos.
And Earth bore starry Heaven, first, to be
An equal to herself, to cover her
All over, and to be a resting-place,
Always secure, for all the blessed gods.
Then she brought forth long hills, the lovely homes
Of goddesses, the Nymphs who live among
The mountain clefts. Then, without pleasant love,
She bore the barren sea with its swollen waves,
Pontus. And then she lay with Heaven, and bore
Deep-whirling Oceanus and Koios; then
Kreius, Iapetos, Hyperion,
Theia, Rhea, Themis, Mnemosyne,
Lovely Tethys, and Phoebe, golden-crowned.
Last, after these, most terrible of sons,
The crooked-scheming Kronos came to birth
Who was his vigorous father's enemy.
Again, she bore the Cyclopes, whose hearts
Were insolent, Brontes and Steropes
And proud-souled Arges, those who found and gave
The thunder and the lightning-bolt to Zeus.
They were like other gods in all respects,
But that a single eye lay in the brow
Of each, and from this, they received the name,
Cyclopes, from the one round eye which lay
Set in the middle of each forehead.⁶ Strength
And energy and craft were in their works.

Then Ouranos and Gaia bore three sons
Mighty and violent, unspeakable
Kottos and Gyes and Briareus,
Insolent children, each with a hundred arms
On his shoulders, darting about, untouchable,
And each had fifty heads, standing upon
His shoulders, over the crowded mass of arms,
And terrible strength was in their mighty forms.

And these most awful sons of Earth and Heaven
Were hated by their father from the first.
As soon as each was born, Ouranos hid
The child in a secret hiding-place in Earth
And would not let it come to see the light,
And he enjoyed this wickedness. But she,
Vast Earth, being strained and stretched inside her, groaned.
And then she thought of a clever, evil plan.
Quickly she made grey adamant,[7] and formed
A mighty sickle, and addressed her sons,
Urging them on, with sorrow in her heart,
'My sons, whose father is a reckless fool,
If you will do as I ask, we shall repay
Your father's wicked crime. For it was he
Who first began devising shameful acts.'

She spoke, but fear seized all of them, and none
Replied. Then crooked Kronos, growing bold,
Answered his well-loved mother with these words:
'Mother, I undertake to do the deed;
I do not care for my unspeakable
Father, for he first thought of shameful acts.'
He spoke, and giant Earth was glad at heart.
She set him in a hiding-place, and put
Into his hands the saw-toothed scimitar,
And told him all the plot she had devised.

Great Heaven came, and with him brought the night.
Longing for love, he lay around the Earth,

28

Spreading out fully. But the hidden boy
Stretched forth his left hand; in his right he took
The great long jagged sickle; eagerly
He harvested his father's genitals
And threw them off behind. They did not fall
From his hands in vain, for all the bloody drops
That leaped out were received by Earth; and when
The year's time was accomplished, she gave birth
To the Furies, and the Giants, strong and huge,
Who fought in shining armour, with long spears,
And the nymphs called Meliae[8] on the broad earth.

The genitals, cut off with adamant
And thrown from land into the stormy sea,
Were carried for a long time on the waves.
White foam surrounded the immortal flesh,
And in it grew a girl. At first it touched
On holy Cythera, from there it came
To Cyprus, circled by the waves. And there
The goddess came forth, lovely, much revered,
And grass grew up beneath her delicate feet.
Her name is Aphrodite among men
And gods, because she grew up in the foam,[9]
And Cytherea, for she reached that land,
And Cyprogenes from the stormy place
Where she was born, and Philommedes[10] from
The genitals, by which she was conceived.
Eros is her companion; fair Desire
Followed her from the first, both at her birth
And when she joined the company of the gods.
From the beginning, both among gods and men,
She had this honour and received this power:
Fond murmuring of girls, and smiles, and tricks,
And sweet delight, and friendliness, and charm.

But the great father Ouranos reproached
His sons, and called them Titans,[11] for, he said

29

They strained in insolence, and did a deed
For which they would be punished afterwards.

And Night bore frightful Doom and the black Ker,[12]
And Death, and Sleep, and the whole tribe of Dreams.

Again, although she slept with none of the gods,
Dark Night gave birth to Blame and sad Distress,
And the Hesperides, who, out beyond
The famous stream of Oceanus, tend
The lovely golden apples, and their trees.
She bore the Destinies and ruthless Fates,
Goddesses who track down the sins of men
And gods, and never cease from awful rage
Until they give the sinner punishment.
Then deadly Night gave birth to Nemesis,
That pain to gods and men, and then she bore
Deceit and Love, sad Age, and strong-willed Strife.
And hateful Strife gave birth to wretched Work,[13]
Forgetfulness, and Famine, tearful Pains,
Battles and Fights, Murders, Killings of men,
Quarrels and Lies and Stories and Disputes,
And Lawlessness and Ruin, both allied,
And Oath, who brings most grief to men on earth
When anyone swears falsely, knowing it.

And Pontus' firstborn child was Nereus,
The honest one, the truthful. The old man
Is called this name because he never errs,[14]
And he is gentle and remembers Right,
And knows the arts of Mercy and the Law.

Then Pontus and Earth produced great Thaumas, proud
Phorkys, and Ceto with her lovely skin,
And Eurybie,[15] with her heart of steel.

And Nereus and Doris, lovely-haired
Daughter of Oceanus, circling stream,

Begot and bore, in the unfruitful sea,
Their children, most beloved of goddesses:[16]
Protho, Eukrante, Sao, Amphitrite,
Eudore, Thetis, Galene, Glauce, and
Cymothoe, Speio, and quick Thalia,
And lovely Pasithea, Erato and
Eunike with her rosy arms, and fair
Melite, Eulimene, Agave,
Doto, Proto, Pherousa, Dynamene,
Nesaia, Aktaia, Protomedeia, and
Doris, Panope, and the beautiful
Galatea, and the lovely Hippothoe,
Rosy-armed Hipponoe, Cymodoce,
Who, acting with trim-ankled Amphitrite
And Cymatolege, easily can still
Waves on the misty sea, and calm the blasts
Of raging winds; Cymo, Eione,
And garlanded Halimede, the one
Who loves to laugh, Glauconome, and next
Pontoporeia, and Leiagore,
Euagore, Laomedeia and
Poulunoe, and then Authonoe,
Lysianassa, and Euarne, lovely-shaped,
Perfect to look at, graceful Psamathe,
Menippe, Neso, and Eupompe; next,
Themisto, Pronoe and Nemertes,
Whose mind is like her deathless father's. These
Are the fifty daughters of blameless Nereus;
And they, as well, are skilled in perfect works.

And Thaumas took Electra for his bride,
Deep-flowing Ocean's daughter, and she bore
Swift Iris and the Harpies; lovely-haired
Aello and Okypete, who fly
On their swift wings as fast as birds, or breath
Of wind; high through the air they hurl themselves.
And Ceto bore to Phorkys the fair-cheeked

Graiae, grey-haired from birth, whom gods and men
Who walk on earth call Grey Ones: Pemphredo
Well-gowned, and Enyo, with yellow robes,
And the Gorgons, they who lived beyond the stream
Of famous Ocean, on the edge near Night,
Where the clear-voiced Hesperides are found.
Their names were Sthenno and Euryale
And Medusa, she who suffered painfully.
Her sisters were immortal, always young,
But she was mortal, and the Dark-haired One[17]
Lay down with her among the flowers of spring
In a soft meadow. And when Perseus
Cut off her head, great Chrysaor sprang out,
And Pegasus the horse, who is so called
Because his birth was near to Ocean's springs;[18]
Chrysaor's name comes from the golden blade[19]
He held when he was born. And Pegasus
Flew from the earth which nurtures sheep, and came
To join the immortal gods. And there he lives
In the house of Zeus, and brings the lightning-shaft
And thunder to wise Zeus. But Chrysaor
Lay with a child of Ocean, Callirhoe,
And fathered Geryon, who had three heads;
The power of Heracles killed Geryon
In sea-surrounded Erythea, near
The shuffling cattle. On that very day
The hero drove the broad-browed cattle home
To holy Tiryns, and crossed Ocean's ford,
And killed the herd Eurytion and the dog
Orthos, in the dark stalls, by Ocean's stream.

She[20] bore another monster, terrible,
In a hollow cave, Echidna, fierce of heart,
Nothing like any mortal man, unlike
Any immortal god, for half of her
Is a fair-cheeked girl with glancing eyes, but half
Is a huge and frightening speckled snake; she eats

Raw flesh in a recess of the holy earth.
Down there she has a cave of hollow rock
Far from the deathless gods and mortal men;
There the gods gave a famous home to her,
And gloomy Echidna keeps her watch down there
Under the ground, among the Arimoi,[21] *tribe?*
A nymph immortal and ageless all her days.

They say that Typho, terrible and proud
And lawless, loved this nymph with glancing eyes, *Echidna—Typho*
And she conceived and bore fierce progeny:
First, Orthos the dog of Geryon, and next,
Unspeakable Cerberus, who eats raw flesh,
The bronze-voiced hound of Hades, shameless, strong,
With fifty heads. And then again she bore
The Lernaean Hydra, skilled in wrong, the one
The goddess white-armed Hera raised, who was
Immensely angry with great Heracles.
With warlike Iolaus' help, and through
The plans of Athene, she who leads the host,
The son of Zeus, Amphitryonides,[22]
Dispatched the Hydra with his ruthless sword.
She[23] bore Chimaera, who breathed awful fire,
Three-headed, frightening, huge, swift-footed, strong,
One head a bright-eyed lion's, one a goat's,
The third a snake's, a mighty dragon-head.
Noble Bellerophon and Pegasus
Caught her. But she, subdued by Orthos, bore
The deadly Sphinx, a curse on the men of Thebes,
And the Nemean lion, a plague to men,
Brought up by Hera, the lady wife of Zeus,
Set down in the Nemean hills to live
Destroying the tribes of men; and he subdued
Nemean Tretus and Apesas. But he
Was conquered by the power of Heracles.
And Ceto, joined in love to Phorkys, bore
Her youngest child, a frightful snake which guards

33

The golden apples, in that secret place
Of the dark earth, at its great boundary-line.
And these are Phorkys' and Ceto's progeny.
Tethys bore whirling Rivers to her mate
Ocean: the Nile, Alpheios, and the deep
Eddying Eridanus, Strymon; then,
Meander, Ister's lovely-flowing stream,
And Phasis, Rhesus, and the silver pools
Of Achelous and Nessus, Rhodius,
Then Haliacmon, Heptaporus, and
Granicus, Aesepus, bright Simois,
Peneus, Hermus, gentle Caicus,
Sangarius the great, Parthenius,
Ladon, Euenus, and Aldescus; last,
She bore Scamander, shining holy stream.

And she bore daughters, holy progeny,
Who, with the Rivers and Apollo, lord,
Have charge of young men over all the earth,
For Zeus appointed them to do this work:
Peitho, Admete, and Ianthe; next,
Electra, Doris, Prymno, and divine
Ourania and Hippo, Clymene,
Rhodeia, Callirhoe, Zeuxo; and
Klutie, Iduia and Pasithoe,
Plexaure, Galaxaure and the loved
Dione, Melobosis, Thoe, fair
Polydore, Kerkeis with lovely shape,
And Pluto with her wide eyes, Perseis,
Ianeira, Akaste, Xanthe and the sweet
Petraie, Menestho, Europe, Metis; next,
Eurynome, Telesto, yellow-robed,
And Chryseis, Asie, lovable
Calypso and Eudore, Tyche, and
Amphiro, and Okuroe and Styx,
Who is the most important one of all.
These are the oldest daughters who were born

To Oceanus and Tethys, but there are
Many others beside them, Oceanids,
Three thousand nymphs with shapely ankles, who
Are scattered everywhere, over the earth
And on deep water, glorious goddesses.
There are as many roaring rivers, too,
Children of Ocean, lady Tethys' sons;
It is hard for mortal man to name their names,
But they are known to those who live nearby.

And Theia, mastered by Hyperion,
Bore Helios the great, bright Selene,
And Eos,[24] who shines upon all men on earth
And on the deathless gods who hold broad heaven.

Eurybie, the shining goddess, joined
In love with Krios, bore to him the great
Astraios, Pallas and Perses, greatly wise.
And with the god Astraios, Eos lay
In love, a goddess herself, and bore the winds
With mighty hearts: the cleansing Zephyros,
And Notos, and swift-racing Boreas.
And Erigeneia[25] brought forth, after these,
The star Eosphoros and all the stars
Which, shining, make a garland for the heavens.[26]

Then Pallas slept with Ocean's daughter, Styx,
Who bore him shapely-ankled Victory
And Glory, in his house, and famous sons:
Power and Force. They have no house apart
From Zeus, nor any seat, nor any path
Except where God commands them, and they sit
Forever at the side of thundering Zeus.[27]
Styx, Ocean's deathless daughter, planned it so,
The day the Lightener of Olympus called
To great Olympus all the deathless gods
And said, whichever of the gods should fight

With him against the Titans would not lose
His honours, but would keep the rights he had
Among the deathless gods up to that day;
And those, he said, who under Kronos had
No rank nor rights would be promoted now
To rank and honours both, as would be just.
And deathless Styx came to Olympus first
And brought her children, as her father advised.
Zeus gave her honour and unequalled gifts:
For she was made the great oath of the gods;
Her children always live at Zeus's side.
And as he promised, Zeus fulfilled his vows
To all; and he rules greatly, and is lord.

And Phoebe came to Koios' longed-for bed.
Loved by the god, the goddess conceived and bore
Leto the dark-robed, always mild and kind
To men and deathless gods; gentlest in all
Olympus; from the beginning, she was mild.
Then Phoebe bore renowned Asterie
Whom Perses led, a bride, to his great house.
Last she bore Hekate,[28] who, above all,
Is honoured by the son of Kronos, Zeus.
He gave her glorious gifts: a share of earth
And of the barren sea. In starry heaven
She has her place, and the immortal gods
Respect her greatly. Even now, when men
Upon the earth, according to the rites,
Make handsome sacrifices, and entreat
The gods for favour, Hekate is called.
Great honours follow readily that man
Whose prayers the goddess graciously receives;
And she can give him wealth; that power is hers.
Of all the children Earth and Ocean bore,
Who once had privilege, she kept her due.
The son of Kronos never did her harm
Nor did he snatch away the rights she had

Under the Titan gods of old; she keeps
Her privilege in earth and sea and heaven
As it was portioned to her from the start.
Nor did she get a lesser share because
She had no brothers to defend her rights.
Her share is greater: Zeus is her advocate.
Help and success come to her favourites;
In court, she sits beside respected lords;
In the assembly of the people, he
Whom she has chosen, shines. And when men arm
For man-destroying war, the goddess helps
The men she wants to help, and eagerly
Brings victory and glorious fame to them.
A splendid ally in the games, when men
Compete, then, too, she brings success and help.
The man she favours wins by might and strength
And gains the lovely prize with ease and joy,
And brings his parents glory. She is good
To stand by horsemen, also good for those
Who work the rude grey sea, and those who pray
To Hekate and to the god who shakes
The earth with crashes, get great hauls from her,
The glorious goddess, if she wishes it,
But just as easily she takes away
All she has given, if she wants it so.
And she is helpful in the stables, too,
Along with Hermes, to increase the stock.
The herds of cattle and of goats, and flocks
Of woolly sheep grow numerous, from few,
If she is willing, or grow small from great.
Thus, among all the honoured, deathless gods
She is revered, although her mother bore
No sons. The son of Kronos also made
Her nurse and overseer of all the young
Who from that day were born and came to see
The light of Dawn who sees the world; and thus
She is a nurse; and these are her high tasks.

37

And Rhea, being forced by Kronos, bore
Most brilliant offspring to him: Hestia,
Demeter, golden-slippered Hera, strong
Hades, who has his home beneath the earth,
The god whose heart is pitiless, and him
Who crashes loudly and who shakes the earth,[29]
And thoughtful Zeus, father of gods and men,
Whose thunder makes the wide earth tremble. Then,
As each child issued from the holy womb
And lay upon its mother's knees, each one
Was seized by mightly Kronos, and gulped down.
He had in mind that no proud son of Heaven
Should hold the royal rank among the gods
Except himself. For he had learned from Earth
And starry Heaven, that his destiny
Was to be overcome, great though he was,
By one of his own sons, and through the plans
Of mighty Zeus. Therefore he never dropped
His guard, but lay in wait, and swallowed down
His children. Rhea suffered endless grief;
But when she was about to bring forth Zeus,
Father of gods and men, she begged the Earth
And starry Heaven, her parents, to devise
A plan to hide the birth of her dear son
And bring the Fury down on Kronos, for
His treatment of his father and his sons
Whom mighty, crooked Kronos swallowed down.
They heard their daughter and agreed, and told
Her all that fate would bring upon the king
Kronos, and to his mighty-hearted son.
They sent her to the fertile land of Crete,
To Lyctus, when she was about to bear
Her youngest child, great Zeus. And in broad Crete
Vast Earth received the child from her, to raise
And cherish. And she carried him, with speed,
Through the black night, and came to Lyctus first.
She took him in her arms and hid him, deep

Under the holy earth, in a vast cave,
On thickly-wooded Mount Aegeum. Then,
To the great lord, the son of Heaven, the past
King of the gods, she handed, solemnly,
All wrapped in swaddling-clothes, a giant stone.
He seized it in his hands and thrust it down
Into his belly, fool! He did not know
His son, no stone, was left behind, unhurt
And undefeated, who would conquer him
With violence and force, and drive him out
From all his honours, and would rule the gods.

The strength and glorious limbs of the young lord
Grew quickly and the years went by, and Earth
Entrapped great clever Kronos with shrewd words
Advising him to bring his offspring back.
(His son, by craft and power, conquered him.)
And first he vomited the stone, which he
Had swallowed last. At holy Pytho, Zeus
Set firm the stone in broad-pathed earth, beneath
Parnassus, in a cleft, to be a sign
In future days, for men to marvel at.

He freed his uncles from their dreadful bonds,
The sons of Heaven; his father, foolishly,
Had bound them. They remembered gratitude
And gave him thunder and the blazing bolt
And lightning, which, before, vast Earth had hid.
Trusting in them, he rules both men and gods.
And Klymene, the lovely-ankled nymph,
Daughter of Ocean, married Iapetos,
And went to bed with him, and bore a son,
Strong-hearted Atlas, then, notorious
Menoitios, and then, Prometheus
Brilliant and shifty, Epimetheus
The foolish one, who first brought harm to men
Who live on bread, for he took Woman in,

39

The manufactured maiden, gift of Zeus.
Far-seeing Zeus cast proud Menoitios
Down into Erebos; he struck him with
The smoking thunderbolt, because he was
Insanely bold and reckless in his pride.
And Atlas, forced by hard necessity,
Holds the broad heaven up, propped on his head
And tireless hands, at the last ends of Earth,
In front of the clear-voiced Hesperides;
For Zeus the Counsellor gave him this fate.
Clever Prometheus was bound by Zeus
In cruel chains, unbreakable, chained round
A pillar, and Zeus roused and set on him
An eagle with long wings, which came and ate
His deathless liver. But the liver grew
Each night, until it made up the amount
The long-winged bird had eaten in the day.
Lovely Alcmene's son, strong Heracles,
Killing the eagle, freed Prometheus
From his affliction and his misery,
And Zeus, Olympian, who rules on high,
Approved, so that the fame of Heracles
The Theban might be greater than before
Upon the fruitful earth; he showed respect,
And gave the honour to his famous son.
And angry though he was, he checked the rage
He felt against Prometheus, who dared
To match his wits against almighty Zeus.

For at Mekone, once, there was a test
When gods and mortal men divided up
An ox; Prometheus audaciously
Set out the portions, trying to deceive
The mind of Zeus. Before the rest, he put
Pieces of meat and marbled inner parts
And fat upon the hide, and hid them in
The stomach of the ox; but before Zeus

The white bones of the ox, arranged with skill,
Hidden in shining fat. And then he spoke,
The father of gods and men, and said to him,
'Milord, most famous son of Iapetos,
The shares you've made, my friend, are most unfair!'
Thus Zeus, whose plans are everlasting, spoke
And criticized. But sly Prometheus
Did not forget his trick, and softly smiled
And said, 'Most glorious Zeus, greatest of all
The gods who live forever, choose your share,
Whichever one your heart leads you to pick.'
He spoke deceitfully, but Zeus who knows
Undying plans, was not deceived, but saw
The trick, and in his heart made plans
To punish mortal men in future days.
He took the fatted portion in his hands
And raged within, and anger seized his heart
To see the trick, the white bones of the ox.
(And from this time the tribes of men on earth
Burn, on the smoking altars, white ox-bones.)

But Zeus, the gatherer of clouds, enraged,
Said, 'Son of Iapetos, cleverest god
Of all: so, friend, you do not yet forget
Your crafty tricks!' So spoke the angry Zeus
Whose craft is everlasting. From that time
He bore the trick in mind, and would not give,
To wretched men who live on earth, the power
Of fire, which never wearies. The brave son
Of Iapetos deceived him, and he stole
The ray, far-seeing, of unwearied fire,
Hid in the hollow fennel stalk, and Zeus
Who thunders in the heavens ate his heart,
And raged within to see the ray of fire
Far-seeing, among men. Immediately
He found a price for men to pay for fire,
An evil: for the famous Limping God 30

Moulded, from earth, the image of a girl
A modest virgin, through the plans of Zeus.
Grey-eyed Athene made her belt and dressed
The girl in robes of silver; over her face
She pulled a veil, embroidered cleverly,
Marvellous to behold, and on her head
Pallas Athene set a lovely wreath
Of blossoms from spring grasses, and a crown
Of gold, made by the famous Limping God,
Worked with his hands, to please his father Zeus.
Upon it many clever things were worked,
Marvellous to behold: monsters which earth
And sea have nourished, made to seem as real
As living, roaring creatures, miracles,
And beauty in abundance shone from it.

When he had made the lovely curse, the price
For the blessing of fire, he brought her to a place
Where gods and men were gathered, and the girl
Was thrilled by all her pretty trappings, given
By mighty Zeus's daughter with grey eyes.
Amazement seized the mortal men and gods,
To see the hopeless trap, deadly to men.

From her comes all the race of womankind,
The deadly female race and tribe of wives
Who live with mortal men and bring them harm,
No help to them in dreadful poverty
But ready enough to share with them in wealth.
As in the covered hive the honey-bees
Keep feeding drones, conspirators in wrong,
And daily, all day long, until the sun
Goes down, the workers hurry about their work
And build white honeycombs, while those inside
In the sheltered storeroom, fill their bellies up
With products of the toil of others, thus,
Women are bad for men, and they conspire
In wrong, and Zeus the Thunderer made it so.

42

He made a second evil as a price
Of fire, man's blessing: if a man avoids
Marriage and all the troubles women bring
And never takes a wife, at last he comes
To miserable old age, and does not have
Anyone who will care for the old man.
He has enough to live on, while he lives,
But when he dies, his distant relatives
Divide his property. The married man
Who gets a good wife, suited to his taste,
Gets good and evil mixed, but he who gets
One of the deadly sort, lives all his life
With never-ending pain inside his heart
And on his mind; the wound cannot be healed.
It is impossible to hoodwink Zeus
Or to surpass him, for Prometheus,
The son of Iapetos, kind though he was
And wise, could not escape his heavy rage
But he was bound by force, with heavy chains.

When Ouranos was angry with his sons
Kottos, Gyes, and Briareus,
At first he bound them up in cruel bonds
Because he envied them their looks and size
And overwhelming masculinity.
He made them live beneath the broad-pathed earth,
And there they suffered, living underground
Farthest away, at great earth's edge; they grieved
For many years, with great pain in their hearts.
The son of Kronos and the other gods
Whom fair-haired Rhea bore to Kronos, took
Gaia's advice, and brought them back to light.
She told them everything: the gods would gain
Glorious pride and victory, with the help
Of those whom they had saved. For Kronos' sons
Had long been fighting, labouring in pain
Against the Titans, in a violent war.

From tall Mount Othrys came the Titan lords
And from Olympus, those who give us all,
Whom fair-haired Rhea bore, after she lay
With Kronos; they had anger in their hearts
And fought continually for ten full years
With no release nor end to the harsh strife
For either side; the winning of the war
Was balanced evenly between the two.
But when the sons of Ouranos received,
Fittingly, nectar and ambrosia, which
The gods themselves consume, their spirits rose
Proud in their breasts. And then the father of gods
And men spoke to them: 'Hear me, glorious sons
Of Ouranos and Gaia, while I speak
As my heart tells me to. For many years
The sons of Kronos and the Titan gods
Have been at war, fighting for victory
And power. Come now, show them your great strength,
Your unapproachable hands, in painful war
Against the Titans, and do not forget
Our kindness and good will, how through our plans
You come back, having suffered, to the light
From gloomy darkness and from painful bonds.'

He spoke, and blameless Kottos answered him:
'You do not need to tell us what we know.
We know your mind and thoughts are excellent
And that you keep the gods from chilly harm.
O Lord and Son of Kronos, we came back
From gloomy darkness and from cruel bonds
Because of your intelligence; we find
An unexpected end to suffering.
Now, with our minds intent, and eager hearts,
We will preserve your power in dreadful war
Against the Titans, on the battlefield.'

He spoke, and all the gods, givers of gifts,
Applauded him, and lusted for the fight

44

Even more than before. And on that day
They joined in hateful battle, all of them,
Both male and female, Titan gods and those
Whom Kronos sired and those whom Zeus had brought
To light from Erebos, beneath the earth,
Strange, mighty ones, whose power was immense,
Each with a hundred arms, darting about,
And each had fifty heads standing upon
His shoulders, over the crowded mass of arms.
They stood against the Titans in the grim
Battle, with giant rocks in their strong hands,
While on their side the Titans eagerly
Strengthened their ranks, and both at once displayed
The mightiest efforts which their hands could make;
The boundless sea roared terribly around,
The great earth rumbled, and broad heaven groaned,
Shaken; and tall Olympus was disturbed
Down to its roots, when the immortals charged.
The heavy quaking from their footsteps reached
Down to dark Tartarus, and piercing sounds
Of awful battle, and their mighty shafts.
They hurled their wounding missiles, and the voice
Of both sides, shouting, reached the starry sky,
And when they met, their ALALE![31] was great.

Then Zeus no longer checked his rage, for now
His heart was filled with fury, and he showed
The full range of his strength. He came from heaven
And from Olympus, lightening as he came,
Continuously; from his mighty hand
The bolts kept flying, bringing thunder-claps
And lightning-flashes, while the holy flame
Rolled thickly all around. The fertile earth
Being burnt, roared out, the voiceless forest cried
And crackled with the fire; the whole earth boiled
And ocean's streams, and the unfruitful sea.
The hot blast reached the earthborn Titans; flame

Unspeakable, rose to the upper air;
The flashing brightness of the thunderbolt
And lightning blinded all, however strong;
The awful heat reached Chaos. To the ear
It sounded, to the eye it looked as though
Broad Heaven were coming down upon the Earth:
For such a noise of crashing might arise
If she were falling, hurled down by his fall.
Just such a mighty crash rose from the gods
Meeting in strife. The howling winds brought on
Duststorm and earthquake, and the shafts of Zeus,
Lightning and thunder and the blazing bolt,
And carried shouting and the battle-cry
Into the armies, and a dreadful noise
Of hideous battle sounded, and their deeds
Were mighty, but the tide of war was turned:
Until that moment, they had kept it up
Continually, in the long, hard fight.

Among those gods who made the fighting harsh
Foremost were Kottos and Briareus
And Gyes, who loved war insatiably.
With their strong hands they hurled three hundred rocks
In quick succession; with their missiles, they
Overshadowed the Titans, put them down
In everlasting shade. Under the earth
Broad-pathed, they sent them, and they bound them up
In painful chains. Proud though the Titans were,
They were defeated by those hands, and sent
To misty Tartarus, as far beneath
The earth, as earth is far beneath the heavens.

An anvil made of bronze, falling from heaven,
Would fall nine nights and days, and on the tenth
Would reach the earth; and if the anvil fell
From earth, would fall again nine nights and days
And come to Tartarus upon the tenth.

A wall of bronze runs around Tartarus,
And round this runs a necklace, triple-thick,
Of purest Night, while up above, there grow
The roots of earth and of the barren sea.
There, in the misty dark, the Titan gods
Are hidden, in a mouldering place, lowest
And last of giant Earth, by the will of Zeus
Who drives the clouds, and they may never leave.
Poseidon set bronze gates upon the place,
And all around it runs the wall; there live
Gyes, Kottos, and Briareus
As faithful guards, for aegis-bearing Zeus.

And there, in order, are the ends and springs
Of gloomy earth and misty Tartarus,
And of the barren sea and starry heaven,
Murky and awful, loathed by the very gods.
There is the yawning mouth of hell, and if
A man should find himself inside the gates
He would not reach the bottom for a year;
Gust after savage gust would carry him
Now here, now there. Even the deathless gods
Find this an awesome mystery. Here, too,
Is found the fearsome home of dismal Night
Hidden in dark blue clouds. Before her house
The son of Iapetos, unshakeable,
Holds up broad heaven with his head and hands
Untiring, in the place where Night and Day
Approach and greet each other, as they cross
The great bronze threshold. When the one goes in
The other leaves; never are both at home,
But always one, outside, crosses the earth,
The other waits at home until her hour
For journeying arrives. The one brings light
All-seeing, to the earth, but deadly Night,
The other, hidden in dark clouds, brings Sleep,
Brother of Death, and carries him in her arms.

47

There live the children of dark Night, dread gods,
Sleep and his brother Death. The shining Sun
Has never looked upon them with his rays
Not going up to heaven, nor coming back.
The one of them is kind to men and goes
Peacefully over earth and the sea's broad back;
The other's heart is iron; in his breast
Is pitiless bronze: if he should touch a man,
That man is his. And even to the gods
Who are immortal, Death is an enemy.

There, further on, the echoing mansion stands
Of mighty Hades, god of the lower world,
And feared Persephone. A monstrous dog
Stands pitiless guard in front, with evil ways:
He wags his tail and both his ears for all
Who enter, but he will not let them go.
Lying in wait he eats up anyone
He catches leaving by the gates of strong
Hades and greatly feared Persephone.

There lives the goddess hated by the gods,
Terrible Styx, the daughter, oldest-born,
Of Ocean, who flows back upon himself.
Far from the gods she has her famous home
Roofed-over with great rocks, and all around
Fixed firm with silver pillars reaching up
To heaven. Seldom does swift Iris come,
Daughter of Thaumas, over the sea's broad back,
To bring a message. But sometimes when fights
And quarrelling arise among the gods
And some one of the gods who have their homes
On Mount Olympus tells a lie, then Zeus
Sends Iris with a golden jug to fetch
The sacred stuff [32] by which gods swear an oath,
The famous chilly water which flows down
From the high precipice. Through the black night

Far under broad-pathed earth, from the holy stream
A branch of Ocean flows; one tenth of him
Is given to her. Winding about the earth
And broad back of the sea, he has nine streams
With silver eddies, and he falls again
Into the salty main; only this one
Flows from a rock, great burden to the gods.

For if one of the gods who hold the peak
Of snowy Mount Olympus, swears an oath
And makes libation falsely, he must lie
Unbreathing, for the period of a year.
No nectar or ambrosia can be his;
He lies without a breath, without a voice,
Covered in bed, hidden in evil trance.
But when his long year of disease is done,
Another, harder trial waits for him:
The gods who are forever shut him out
Nine years; he never joins their banqueting
Or councils, nine full years. But in the tenth
He enters the assembly of the gods
Immortal, who possess Olympian homes.
Such is the oath the gods have fixed: to swear
On the primeval water of the Styx
Which never fails, but leaps out from the rocks.

And there, in order, are the ends and springs
Of gloomy earth and misty Tartarus,
And of the barren sea and starry heaven,
Murky and awful, loathed by the very gods.
There are the shining gates, the threshold, bronze,
Unshakeable, whose roots are infinite
Forever fixed, for bronze grows in that place.
And further on, apart from all the gods,
The Titans live, out beyond Chaos' gloom.
The famous allies of wide-thundering Zeus
Kottos and Gyes, have their dwelling-place

49

At Ocean's source. But brave Briareus
Was made the son-in-law of him who roars
Deeply, the Shaker of the Earth: he gave
His daughter Cymopolea as his bride.

After Zeus drove the Titans out of heaven
Vast Earth loved Tartarus, and bore a child,
Her last, through golden Aphrodite's work,
Typhoeus, mighty god, whose hands were strong
And feet untiring. On his shoulders grew
A hundred snaky heads, strange dragon heads
With black tongues darting out. His eyes flashed fire
Beneath the brows upon those heads, and fire
Blazed out from every head when he looked round.
Astounding voices came from those weird heads,
All kinds of voices: sometimes speech which gods
Would understand, and sometimes bellowings,
As of a bull let loose, enraged, and proud,
Sometimes that of a ruthless lion; then,
Sometimes the yelp of puppies, marvellous
To hear; and then sometimes he hissed,
And the tall mountains echoed underneath.

Surely that day a thing beyond all help
Might have occurred: he might have come to rule
Over the gods and mortal man, had not
The father of gods and men been quick to see
The danger; but he thundered mightily
And fiercely, and the earth rang terribly,
Broad heaven above, the sea, and Ocean's streams
And Tartarus resounded. As the lord
Arose, mighty Olympus shook beneath
The immortal feet, and Earth gave out a groan.
The purple sea was seized by heat from both,
From thunder and from lightning, and from fire
The monster bore: the burning hurricane
And blazing thunderbolt. The whole earth boiled

And heaven and the sea. The great waves raged
Along the shore, at the immortal's charge,
And endless quakes arose. Hades, the lord
Of dead men down below, trembled for fear,
And the Titans, they who live with Kronos, down
Under Tartarus, shook at the endless din
And fearful battle. Zeus raised up his strength
Seizing his arms, lightning, the blazing bolt,
And thunder, leaped down from Olympus, struck,
And burned the dreadful monster's ghastly heads.
He lashed him with a whip and mastered him,
And threw him down, all maimed, and great Earth groaned.
A flame leaped from the lightning-blasted lord,
When he was struck, on the jagged mountainside.
Great earth was widely scorched by the awful blast
And melted, as tin melts when, skilfully,
Men heat it in the hollow crucibles
Of iron, which is strongest of all things,
But can be conquered by the blazing fire
In mountain hollows, in the holy earth,
And melts, under Hephaistos' clever hands:
Thus earth was melted in the fire's bright flash.
And, angry in his heart, Zeus hurled him down
To Tartarus. And from Typhoeus come
The fierce, rain-blowing winds – not Boreas
Or Notos or bright Zephyros, for these
Come from the gods, and they refresh mankind –
But others, reckless gusts, blow on the sea;
Some fall upon the misty sea and bring
Calamity to men; as evil storms
They rage; each blows in season, scattering ships
And killing sailors. Men who meet with them
At sea have no defence against their power.
And sometimes over the vast and blooming earth
They blast the lovely fields of earthborn men
And fill the land with dust and dreadful noise.
But when the blessed gods had done their work

And forcibly put down the Titans' claim
To honour, they fulfilled Earth's plans and urged
Far-seeing Zeus, Olympian, to rule
And be the king of the immortals. Thus
He gave out rank and privilege to each.

Now Zeus, king of the gods, first took to wife
Metis, wisest of all, of gods and men.
But when she was about to bear her child
Grey-eyed Athene, he deceived her mind
With clever words and guile, and thrust her down
Into his belly, as he was advised
By Earth and starry Heaven. In that way
They said, no other god than Zeus would get
The royal power over all the gods
Who live forever. For her fate would be
To bear outstanding children, greatly wise,
First, a girl, Tritogeneia,³³ the grey-eyed,
Equal in spirit and intelligence
To Zeus her father; then she would bear a son
With haughty heart, a king of gods and men.
But Zeus, forestalling danger, put her down
Into his belly, so that the goddess could
Counsel him in both good and evil plans.³⁴
And shining Themis was his second wife.
She bore the Horae:³⁵ Order, blooming Peace,
And Justice, who attend the works of men,
And then the Fates, to whom wise Zeus has paid
The greatest honour: Clotho, Atropos,
Lachesis, who give men all good and bad.

The daughter of Ocean, fair Eurynome,
Next bore to him three daughters, the fair-cheeked
Graces, Aglaia and Euphrosyne,
And lovely Thalia. From their glancing eyes
Flowed love that melts the strength of a man's limbs,
Their gaze, beneath their brows, is beautiful.

Demeter, who feeds all, came to the bed
Of Zeus, and bore white-armed Persephone,
Whom Aidoneus stole away from her,
But Zeus the counsellor approved the match.

Again, he loved fair-haired Mnemosyne, *memory?*
Who bore the Muses, golden-crowned, the Nine,
Whose pleasure is in feasting and sweet song.

And Leto joined in love with Zeus who holds
The aegis, and the offspring which she bore
Were lovelier than all the sons of Heaven:
Apollo and the huntress Artemis.
Last he took blooming Hera for his wife;
Uniting with the king of gods and men,
She gave him Hebe and Ares, and she bore
The goddess Eileithuia to her mate.

But Zeus himself produced, from his own head,
Grey-eyed Athene, fearsome queen who brings
The noise of war and, tireless, leads the host,
She who loves shouts and battling and fights.
Then Hera, angry, quarrelled with her mate
And bore, without the act of love, a son
Hephaistos, famous for his workmanship,
More skilled in crafts than all the sons of Heaven.

Amphitrite and He who Shakes the Earth,
The crashing god, produced a mighty son,
Wide-ruling Triton, he who holds the deep,
A fearsome god, who lives in a golden house
Beside his mother and the lord
His father. And to Ares, who pierces shields,
Cytherea bore Terror and Fear, dread gods
Who come with Ares, sacker of towns, and spread
Confusion in the close-packed ranks of men
In numbing war; then Cytherea bore

Harmonia, bold-hearted Cadmus' wife.
And Maia, daughter of Atlas, came to Zeus
And to his holy bed, and bore to him
Glorious Hermes, herald of the gods.

Semele, Cadmus' daughter, lay with Zeus
And bore to him a brilliant son, a god,
Glad Dionysus, mortal though she was,
And now they both have joined the ranks of gods.

Alcmene, lying in love with Zeus, who drives
The clouds, gave birth to Heracles the strong.

The famous limping god, Hephaistos, made
Aglaia, youngest Grace, his blooming wife.
And golden Dionysus took to wife
The fair-haired Ariadne, Minos' child:
The son of Kronos saved her from death and age.

And then strong Heracles, the glorious son
Of trim-ankled Alcmene, at the end
Of all his painful labours, made his bride
Hebe, the modest child of mighty Zeus
And golden-slippered Hera, on snow-clad
Olympus. Happy god! For he has done
His great work and he lives among the gods
Forever young, forever free from pain.
The famous daughter of Ocean, Perseis,
Bore to her mate, untiring Helios,
Circe and King Aeëtes. He, the son
Of Helios, who brings light to mortal men,
Was married to Iduia the fair-cheeked
Daughter of Ocean, earth's last stream, by will
Of the immortals, and subdued by love
Through golden Aphrodite's work, she bore
To him Medea with the graceful feet.

And now, farewell, Olympians, and you
Islands and continents and salty sea;
Now sing, Olympian Muses, daughters of Zeus
Who holds the aegis, sing the company
Of goddesses who lay with mortal men
And bore them children who were like the gods.

Demeter, shining goddess, joined in love
With Iasion the hero, on the rich
Island of Crete; they lay on fallow land
Which had been ploughed three times, and she gave birth
To Ploutos, splendid god who travels far
Over the land, and on the sea's broad back;
And everyone who meets or touches him
Grows wealthy, for great riches come from him.
To Cadmus, golden Aphrodite's child
Harmonia was married and she bore
Ino and Semele, and the fair-cheeked
Agave, and Autonoe, the wife
Of Aristaeus with the flowing hair,
And Polydorus, in high-towered Thebes.

Callirhoe, the daughter of Ocean, joined
In golden Aphrodite's love with strong
Chrysaor, and she bore a son to him,
Strongest of mortals, Geryones, he
Whom mighty Heracles subdued and killed
To avenge his cattle with their shuffling feet,
On Erytheia, circled by the sea.

And to Tithonus Eos bore two sons
Memnon, the king of Ethiopia,
Bronze-helmeted, and lord Emathion.
To Kephalos she bore a brilliant son,
Strong Phaethon, a man much like the gods.
When he was young and had the fragile bloom
Of glorious youth, and tender, childish mind,

55

The laughter-loving Aphrodite seized
And took him to her shrine and made him serve
As temple-keeper, bright divinity.
And by the will of the immortal gods
The son of Aeson took Aeëtes' child
From her father, King Aeëtes, loved by Zeus.
The great king, overbearing Pelias,
Outrageous, proud and vicious, ordered him,
The son of Aeson, to accomplish tasks,
Great, painful labours, but he finished them,
And having laboured long, the job complete,
He came to Iolcus in his speedy ship
And made the bright-eyed girl his blooming wife.
Subdued by Jason, shepherd of the folk,
She bore Medeius, and the boy was raised
By Cheiron, son of Philyra, in the hills;
And so the will of great Zeus was fulfilled.

A daughter of the Old Man of the Sea,
Psamathe, shining goddess, through the work
Of golden Aphrodite, fell in love
With Aeacus, and Phocus was her child.
And Thetis, another child of Nereus,
The silver-slippered goddess, was subdued
By Peleus, and bore a son to him
Lion-hearted Achilles, breaker of men.

And fair-crowned Cytherea felt sweet love
For the hero Anchises, and she lay with him
And bore Aeneas on the mountaintop,
In Ida, with its many wooded clefts.

And Circe, daughter of Helios, the son
Of Hyperion, loved Odysseus, patient-souled,
And bore great good Latinus and Agrius.
And they, in the midst of holy islands, ruled
The famous Tyrsenians, so far away.

Calypso, shining goddess, felt sweet love
For Odysseus, and lay with him, and bore to him
Nausithoos and Nausinoos, two sons.

These are the goddesses who lay with men
And bore them children who were like the gods.
Now sing of women, Muses, you sweet-voiced
Olympian daughters of aegis-bearing Zeus: [36]

Hesiod, *Works and Days*

PIERIAN Muses, bringers of fame: come
Tell of your father, Zeus, and sing his hymn,
Through whom each man is famous or unknown,
Talked-of or left obscure, through his great will.
With ease he strengthens any man; with ease
He makes the strong man humble and with ease
He levels mountains and exalts the plain,
Withers the proud and makes the crooked straight
With ease, the Thunderer whose home is high.
Hear, Zeus, and set our fallen laws upright
And may my song to Perses tell the truth.

Strife is no only child. Upon the earth
Two Strifes exist; the one is praised by those
Who come to know her, and the other blamed.
Their natures differ: for the cruel one
Makes battles thrive, and war; she wins no love
But men are forced, by the immortals' will,
To pay the grievous goddess due respect.
The other, first-born child of blackest Night,
Was set by Zeus, who lives in air, on high,
Set in the roots of earth, an aid to men.
She urges even lazy men to work:
A man grows eager, seeing another rich
From ploughing, planting, ordering his house;
So neighbour vies with neighbour in the rush
For wealth: this Strife is good for mortal men –
Potter hates potter, carpenters compete,
And beggar strives with beggar, bard with bard.

59

O Perses, store this in your heart; do not
Let Wicked Strife persuade you, skipping work,
To gape at politicians and give ear
To all the quarrels of the market place.
He has no time for courts and public life
Who has not stored up one full year's supply
Of corn, Demeter's gift, got from the earth.
When you have grain piled high, you may dispute
And fight about the goods of other men.
But *you* will never get this chance again:
Come, let us settle our dispute at once,
And let our judge be Zeus, whose laws are just.
We split our property in half, but you
Grabbed at the larger part and praised to heaven
The lords who love to try a case like that,
Eaters of bribes. The fools! They do not know
That half may be worth more by far than whole,
Nor how much profit lies in poor man's bread.[1]

The gods desire to keep the stuff of life
Hidden from us. If they did not, you could
Work for a day and earn a year's supplies;
You'd pack away your rudder, and retire
The oxen and the labouring mules. But Zeus
Concealed the secret, angry in his heart
At being hoodwinked by Prometheus,
And so he thought of painful cares for men.
First he hid fire. But the son of Iapetos[2]
Stole it from Zeus the Wise, concealed the flame
In a fennel stalk, and fooled the Thunderer.

Then, raging, spoke the Gatherer of Clouds:
'Prometheus, most crafty god of all,
You stole the fire and tricked me, happily,
You, plague on all mankind and on yourself.
They'll pay for fire: I'll give another gift
To men, an evil thing for their delight,

And all will love this ruin in their hearts.'
So spoke the father of men and gods, and laughed.

He told Hephaistos quickly to mix earth
And water, and to put in it a voice
And human power to move, to make a face
Like an immortal goddess, and to shape
The lovely figure of a virgin girl.
Athene was to teach the girl to weave,
And golden Aphrodite to pour charm
Upon her head, and painful, strong desire,
And body-shattering cares. Zeus ordered, then,
The killer of Argos, Hermes, to put in
Sly manners, and the morals of a bitch.
The son of Kronos spoke, and was obeyed.
The Lame God moulded earth as Zeus decreed
Into the image of a modest girl,
Grey-eyed Athene made her robes and belt,
Divine Seduction and the Graces gave
Her golden necklaces, and for her head
The Seasons wove spring flowers into a crown.
Hermes the Messenger put in her breast
Lies and persuasive words and cunning ways;
The herald of the gods then named the girl
Pandora,[3] for the gifts which all the gods
Had given her, this ruin of mankind.

The deep and total trap was now complete;
The Father sent the gods' fast messenger
To bring the gift to Epimetheus.[4]
And Epimetheus forgot the words
His brother said, to take no gift from Zeus,
But send it back, lest it should injure men.
He took the gift, and understood, too late.

Before this time men lived upon the earth
Apart from sorrow and from painful work,

Free from disease, which brings the Death-gods in.
But now the woman opened up the cask,
And scattered pains and evils among men.
Inside the cask's hard walls remained one thing,
Hope,⁵ only, which did not fly through the door.
The lid stopped her, but all the others flew,
Thousands of troubles, wandering the earth.
The earth is full of evils, and the sea.
Diseases come to visit men by day
And, uninvited, come again at night
Bringing their pains in silence, for they were
Deprived of speech by Zeus the Wise. And so
There is no way to flee the mind of Zeus.

And now with art and skill I'll summarize
Another tale, which you should take to heart,
Of how both gods and men began the same.
The gods, who live on Mount Olympus, first
Fashioned a golden race of mortal men;
These lived in the reign of Kronos, king of heaven,
And like the gods they lived with happy hearts
Untouched by work or sorrow. Vile old age
Never appeared, but always lively-limbed,
Far from all ills, they feasted happily.
Death came to them as sleep, and all good things
Were theirs; ungrudgingly, the fertile land
Gave up her fruits unasked. Happy to be
At peace, they lived with every want supplied,
[Rich in their flocks, dear to the blessed gods.]

And then this race was hidden in the ground.
But still they live as spirits of the earth,
Holy and good, guardians who keep off harm,
Givers of wealth: this kingly right is theirs.
The gods, who live on Mount Olympus, next
Fashioned a lesser, silver race of men:
Unlike the gold in stature or in mind.

A child was raised at home a hundred years
And played, huge baby, by his mother's side.
When they were grown and reached their prime, they lived
Brief, anguished lives, from foolishness, for they
Could not control themselves, but recklessly
Injured each other and forsook the gods;
They did not sacrifice, as all tribes must, but left
The holy altars bare. And, angry, Zeus
The son of Kronos, hid this race away,
For they dishonoured the Olympian gods.

The earth then hid this second race, and they
Are called the spirits of the underworld,
Inferior to the gold, but honoured, too.
And Zeus the father made a race of bronze,
Sprung from the ash tree,[6] worse than the silver race,
But strange and full of power. And they loved
The groans and violence of war; they ate
No bread; their hearts were flinty-hard; they were
Terrible men; their strength was great, their arms
And shoulders and their limbs invincible.
Their weapons were of bronze, their houses bronze;
Their tools were bronze: black iron was not known.
They died by their own hands, and nameless, went
To Hades' chilly house. Although they were
Great soldiers, they were captured by black Death,
And left the shining brightness of the sun.

But when this race was covered by the earth,
The son of Kronos made another, fourth,
Upon the fruitful land, more just and good,
A godlike race of heroes, who are called
The demi-gods – the race before our own.
Foul wars and dreadful battles ruined some;
Some sought the flocks of Oedipus, and died
In Cadmus' land, at seven-gated Thebes;
And some, who crossed the open sea in ships,

For fair-haired Helen's sake, were killed at Troy.
These men were covered up in death, but Zeus
The son of Kronos gave the others life
And homes apart from mortals, at Earth's edge.
And there they live a carefree life, beside
The whirling Ocean, on the Blessed Isles.
Three times a year the blooming, fertile earth
Bears honeyed fruits for them, the happy ones.
[And Kronos is their king, far from the gods,
For Zeus released him from his bonds, and these,
The race of heroes, well deserve their fame.

Far-seeing Zeus then made another race,
The fifth, who live now on the fertile earth.]
I wish I were not of this race, that I
Had died before, or had not yet been born.
This is the race of iron. Now, by day,
Men work and grieve unceasingly; by night,
They waste away and die. The gods will give
Harsh burdens, but will mingle in some good;
Zeus will destroy this race of mortal men,
When babies shall be born with greying hair.
Father will have no common bond with son,
Neither will guest with host, nor friend with friend;
The brother-love of past days will be gone.
Men will dishonour parents, who grow old
Too quickly, and will blame and criticize
With cruel words. Wretched and godless, they
Refusing to repay their bringing up,
Will cheat their aged parents of their due.
Men will destroy the towns of other men.
The just, the good, the man who keeps his word
Will be despised, but men will praise the bad
And insolent. Might will be Right, and shame
Will cease to be. Men will do injury
To better men by speaking crooked words
And adding lying oaths; and everywhere

Harsh-voiced and sullen-faced and loving harm,
Envy will walk along with wretched men.
Last, to Olympus from the broad-pathed Earth,
Hiding their loveliness in robes of white,
To join the gods, abandoning mankind,
Will go the spirits Righteousness and Shame.[7]
And only grievous troubles will be left
For men, and no defence against our wrongs.

And now, for lords who understand, I'll tell
A fable: once a hawk, high in the clouds,
Clutched in his claws a speckled nightingale.
She, pierced by those hooked claws, cried, 'Pity me!'
But he made scornful answer: 'Silly thing.
Why do you cry? Your master holds you fast,
You'll go where I decide, although you have
A minstrel's lovely voice, and if I choose,
I'll have you for a meal, or let you go.
Only a fool will match himself against
A stronger party, for he'll only lose,
And be disgraced as well as beaten.' Thus
Spoke the swift-flying hawk, the long-winged bird.

O Perses, follow right; control your pride.
For pride is evil in a common man.
Even a noble finds it hard to bear;
It weighs him down and leads him to disgrace.
The road to justice is the better way,
For Justice in the end will win the race
And Pride will lose: the simpleton must learn
This fact through suffering. The god of Oaths
Runs faster than a crooked verdict; when
Justice is dragged out of the way by men
Who judge dishonestly and swallow bribes,
A struggling sound is heard; then she returns
Back to the city and the homes of men,
Wrapped in a mist and weeping, and she brings

65

Harm to the crooked men who drove her out.
But when the judges of a town are fair
To foreigner and citizen alike,
Their city prospers and her people bloom;
Since Peace is in the land, her children thrive;
Zeus never marks them out for cruel war.
Famine and blight do not beset the just,
Who till their well-worked fields and feast. The earth
Supports them lavishly; and on the hills
The oak bears acorns for them at the top
And honey-bees below; their woolly sheep
Bear heavy fleeces, and their wives bear sons
Just like their fathers. Since they always thrive,
They have no need to go on ships, because
The plenty-bringing land gives them her fruit.

But there are some who till the fields of pride
And work at evil deeds; Zeus marks them out,
And often, all the city suffers for
Their wicked schemes, and on these men, from heaven
The son of Kronos sends great punishments,
Both plague and famine, and the people die.
Their wives are barren, and their villages
Dwindle, according to the plan of Zeus.
At other times the son of Kronos will
Destroy their army, or will snatch away
Their city wall, or all their ships at sea.
You lords, take notice of this punishment.
The deathless gods are never far away;
They mark the crooked judges who grind down
Their fellow-men and do not fear the gods.
Three times ten thousand watchers-over-men,
Immortal, roam the fertile earth for Zeus.
Clothed in a mist, they visit every land
And keep a watch on law-suits and on crimes.
One of them is the virgin, born of Zeus,
Justice, revered by all the Olympian gods.

Whenever she is hurt by perjurers,
Straightway she sits beside her father Zeus,
And tells him of the unjust hearts of men,
Until the city suffers for its lords
Who recklessly, with mischief in their minds,
Pervert their judgements crookedly. Beware,
You lords who swallow bribes, and try to judge
Uprightly, clear your minds of crookedness.
He hurts himself who hurts another man,
And evil planning harms the planner most.

The eye of Zeus sees all, and understands,
And when he wishes, marks and does not miss
How just a city is, inside. And I
Would not myself be just, nor have my son
Be just among bad men: for it is bad
To be an honest man where felons rule;
I trust wise Zeus to save me from this pass.
But you, O Perses, think about these things;
Follow the just, avoiding violence.
The son of Kronos made this law for men:
That animals and fish and winged birds
Should eat each other, for they have no law.
But mankind has the law of Right from him,
Which is the better way. And if one knows
The law of Justice and proclaims it, Zeus
Far-seeing gives one great prosperity.
But if a man, with knowledge, swears an oath
Committing perjury and harming right
Beyond repair, his family will be cursed
In after times, and come to nothing. He
Who keeps his oath will benefit his house.

I say important things for you to hear,
O foolish Perses: Badness can be caught
In great abundance, easily; the road
To her is level, and she lives near by.

But Good is harder, for the gods have placed
In front of her much sweat; the road is steep
And long and rocky at the first, but when
You reach the top, she is not hard to find.

That man is best who reasons for himself,
Considering the future. Also good
Is he who takes another's good advice.
But he who neither thinks himself nor learns
From others, is a failure as a man.

O noble Perses, keep my words in mind,
And work till Hunger is your enemy
And till Demeter, awesome, garlanded,
Becomes your friend and fills your granary.
For Hunger always loves a lazy man;
Both gods and men despise him, for he is
Much like the stingless drone, who does not work
But eats, and wastes the effort of the bees.
But you must learn to organize your work
So you may have full barns at harvest time.
From working, men grow rich in flocks and gold
And dearer to the deathless gods. In work
There is no shame; shame is in idleness.
And if you work, the lazy man will soon
Envy your wealth: a rich man can become
Famous and good. No matter what your luck,
To work is better; turn your foolish mind
From other men's possessions to your own,
And earn your living, as I tell you to.
A cringing humbleness accompanies
The needy man, a humbleness which may
Destroy or profit him. The humble are
The poor men, while the rich are self-assured.
Money should not be seized; that gold which is
God's gift is better. If a man gets wealth
By force of hands or through his lying tongue,

As often happens, when greed clouds his mind
And shame is pushed aside by shamelessness,
Then the gods blot him out and blast his house
And soon his wealth deserts him. Also, he
Who harms a guest or suppliant, or acts
Unseemly, sleeping with his brother's wife,
Or in his folly, hurts an orphan child,
Or he who picks rough quarrels, and attacks
His father at the threshold of old age,
He angers Zeus himself, and in the end
He pays harsh penalties for all his sins.

Now, shut your foolish heart against these things
And sacrifice to the immortal gods
With reverence and ritual cleanliness,
And burn the glorious thigh-bones; please the gods
With incense and libations, when you go
To bed, and when the holy light returns,
That they may favour you, with gracious hearts
And spirits, so that you may buy the lands
Of other men, and they may not buy yours.

Invite your friend, but not your enemy,
To dine; especially, be cordial to
Your neighbour, for if trouble comes at home,
A neighbour's there, at hand; while kinsmen take
Some time to arm themselves. It is a curse
To have a worthless neighbour; equally,
A good one is a blessing; he who is
So blest possesses something of great worth.
No cow of yours will stray away if you
Have watchful neighbours. Measure carefully
When you must borrow from your neighbour, then,
Pay back the same, or more, if possible,
And you will have a friend in time of need.

Shun evil profit, for dishonest gain
Is just the same as failure. Love your friends;

Approach the men who come to you, and give
To him who gives, but not, if he does not.
We give to generous men, but no one gives
To stingy ones. Give is a lovely girl,
But Grab is bad, and she gives only death.
The man who gives ungrudgingly is glad
At heart, rejoicing in his gift, but if
A man forgets his shame and takes something,
However small, his heart grows stiff and cold.

Add to your stores, and Famine, burning-eyed,
Will stay away. Even if your supply
Is small, and if you add a little bit,
And do it often, soon it will be big.
Less worry comes from having wealth at home;
Business abroad is always insecure.

Think about this: to draw on what you have
Is fine; to need and have not pains the heart.

Be sparing of the middle of a cask,
But when you open it, and at the end,
Drink all you want; it's not worth saving dregs.

Let wages promised to a friend be fixed
Beforehand; even with your brother, smile
And have a witness, for too much mistrust
And too much trust can both be ruinous.

Don't let a woman, wiggling her behind,
And flattering and coaxing, take you in;
She wants your barn: woman is just a cheat.

An only son preserves his father's name
And keeps the fortune growing in one house;
If you have two, you'll need to have more wealth
And live a longer time. But Zeus can find

Ways to enrich a larger family:
More children mean more help and greater gains.

If in your heart you pray for riches, do
These things; pile work on work, and still more work.

When the Pleiads, Atlas' daughters, start to rise [8]
Begin your harvest; plough when they go down. [9]
For forty days and nights they hide themselves,
And as the year rolls round, appear again
When you begin to sharpen sickle-blades;
This law holds on the plains and by the sea,
And in the mountain valleys, fertile lands
Far from the swelling sea. To sow your seed
Go naked; strip to plough and strip to reap,
If you would harvest all Demeter's yield
In season. Thus each crop will come in turn,
And later, you will not be found in need
And forced to beg from other men, and get
No help. See now, you come to me like that,
And I will neither give nor lend to you.
You foolish Perses, go to work! The gods
Have given work to men; don't let it be
That you should take your children and your wife
And beg, with downcast spirit, for your food
From neighbours who refuse to care. You may
Succeed two times or three. But after that,
You'll bother them in vain, and all your words
Will come to nothing, and your arguments
Will fail. I ask you, think about this way
To banish hunger, and to pay your debts:

First, get a house, a woman, and an ox
For ploughing – let the woman be a slave,
Unmarried, who can help you in the fields,
Make ready in your house the things you'll need,
So you won't have to try to borrow tools

71

And be refused, and do without, and let
The ripe time pass and all your work be lost.
Don't put off work until another day,
Or even till tomorrow; lazy men
Who put things off always have unfilled barns.
Constant attention makes the work go well;
Idlers wrestle with ruin all their days.

The sun's sharp fury and the drenching heat
Subside, and mighty Zeus sends autumn rain,
Our bodies move more nimbly; then, by day,
Sirius passes overhead less time[10]
And travels more at night. The tree you cut
At this time, when it sheds its leaves and stops
Sprouting, will be most free of wormholes. Now
The time for cutting timber has arrived.
Your grinding-mortar should be three feet deep;[11]
Four and a half will make your pestle; next,
Your axle should be seven, that will do,
But with an eight-foot length you'll have enough
To make a mallet-head, for breaking clods.
Your wagon-wheels should be about two feet
Across to fit a wagon ten palms wide.
The wood that is not straight can still be used
For fuel; bring a lot of it, and bring
A curving plough-beam when you come on one.
Look for it on the farm or in the hills;
The holm-oak makes the strongest plough-beam when
One of Athene's craftsmen fits it to
The stock, and fastens on the pole. It's best
To make two ploughs at home, for if one breaks,
You'll have the other for your oxen. Elm
Or laurel make the soundest poles; the stock
Should be of oak, the beam of holm-oak. Get
Two nine-year-old bull oxen. In their prime,
They have full strength, and work the best, nor will
They quarrel in the furrows, break the plough,

And leave the work unfinished. After them
Should go a vigorous forty-year-old hand,
Who'll dine upon a quartered, eight-slice loaf.[12]
Who'll do his job and drive the furrows straight,
Who'll keep his mind on work, not look around
For friends, the way a young man would. He'll sow
With care, not wasting seed; less stable men
Get flustered, dreaming of their social life.

The crane, returning every year, cries out[13]
From the clouds above, and when you hear her voice,
Know that she means the time has come to plough,
The time of chilly rains. She gnaws the hearts
Of men who have no oxen. Now's the time
You'll need some bent-horned oxen of your own,
Fattened at home. It's easy, then, to say
'Bring me my pair and wagon;' easy, too,
To turn a neighbour down: 'My oxen have
Their work to do.' The man who's rich in mind
Alone believes his wagon's all but built,
The fool! He doesn't know a hundred boards
Are needed for a wagon: take some pains
And get, beforehand, everything you'll need.

When ploughing-time arrives, make haste to plough,
You and your slaves alike, on rainy days
And dry ones, while the season lasts. At dawn
Get to your fields, and one day they'll be full.
Plough, too, in springtime; if you turn the earth
In summer, too, you won't regret the work.
Sow fallow soil while it is still quite light;
Remember, fallow land defends us all,
And lulls our children with security.
Make prayers to Zeus the farmer's god and to
Holy Demeter, for her sacred grain,
To make it ripe and heavy, when you start
To plough, and hold the handles in your hand,

And strike the oxen as they tug the straps.
A slave should follow after, with a stick
To hide the seeds and disappoint the birds.
Good habits are man's finest friend, and bad
Are his worst enemy. If you proceed
As I've described, your corn will nod and bow
With fatness, to the ground, if Zeus himself
Gives, finally, a happy issue. Then,
You'll sweep the cobwebs from your storage jars,
And you'll be glad, I think, to have your food
Stored up to draw on. Till pale spring arrives,
You'll have your fill, not stare at other men,
But other men will come to *you* in need.

But if you put off ploughing till the Sun
Has reached his winter turning-point,[14] you'll reap
Sitting, and grasp your little crop, and bind
In dusty haste, and unrejoicing haul
Your harvest in a basket: few will cheer.

But Zeus who holds the aegis has a mind
Unknowable for men and changeable.
And though you've ploughed too late, this cure may come:
When first the cuckoo calls among the oaks[15]
And pleases men over the boundless earth,
If, from the third day, Zeus sends constant rain
Until the water rises to a point
No higher than an ox's hoof but not
Much lower, then the farmer who ploughed late
May rival him who did the job on time.
Keep all these things in mind; anticipate
Grey springtime, and the rainy time of year.

Pass by the blacksmith's busy shop, the crowd
Of gossipers in winter, when the cold
Keeps men from work, for then a busy man
Can benefit his house: do not be caught

74

Helpless and poor in cruel wintertime,
Rubbing your swollen feet with scrawny hands.
The idle man who lives on empty hope
And has no way to earn his living, turns
His mind to crime: hope is not good for him
Who sits and gossips when he has no job.

When summer still is waxing, tell your slaves:
'Summer is not for ever; now, build barns.'

Defend yourself against the evil days
Lenaion[16] brings, all of them days which pierce
The hides of oxen; guard against the frosts
That kill, when Boreas blows on the earth.
He blows through Thrace, where horses graze; he blows
On the broad sea and whips it up: the earth
And forest mutter; in the mountain pass
He falls on high-leafed oaks and thick-branched pines
And brings them to the fruitful earth; while all
The boundless forests cry. The animals
Shudder, with tails between their legs; they find
No help in furry hides, the cold goes through
Even the shaggy-breasted. Boreas
Goes through an ox's hide, through the fine coat
The goat wears, but his windy force cannot
Pierce through the thick-piled fleece of sheep; he makes
The old man bend, round-shouldered as a wheel.
He does not pierce the soft-skinned girl who stays
Indoors at home with mother, innocent
Of golden Aphrodite's works. She bathes
Her tender skin, anoints herself with oil,
And going to an inner room at home,
She takes a nap upon a winter day,
When, in his fireless house and dismal place
The Boneless One[17] is gnawing on his foot.
For him, the sun no longer lights the way
To better feeding grounds: the sun has gone

To make his circuit with the dark-skinned men;[18]
He shines upon the Greeks a shorter time.
The horned and hornless creatures of the wood
In pain, with chattering teeth, flee through the brush,
One care in all their minds, to find a cave
Or thickly covered shelter. Like the man,
Three-legged with his staff, with shattered spine,
Whose head looks to the ground, like him they go
Wandering, looking for shelter from the snow.

Then put your body in a shelter too:
A fleecy coat and tunic to the ground,
Woven with thicker woof than warp; do this
So that your body's hair lies still and does
Not shudder and stand up all over. Next,
Bind on your feet the fitted oxhide boots,
Lined with thick felt. And when the chilly time
Approaches, stitch the hides of newborn kids
With sinews from an ox, into a cape
To keep the rain from falling on your back.
A fitted cap of felt upon your head
Keeps your ears dry; when Boreas attacks
The dawn is cold. From starry heaven at dawn
A fruitful mist is spread upon the earth
Upon the lucky fields. The mist is drawn
From ever-flowing rivers; stormy winds
Force it up high above the earth; sometimes
It falls as rain at evening, other times
It turns to wind when Thracian Boreas
Stirs up the thick-massed clouds. Finish your work;
Get home ahead of him, so you will not
Be swallowed up in that black cloud from heaven
And come home dripping, with your clothing soaked.
Be on your guard: this is the hardest month,
Stormy, hard on the stock and hard on men.
Your oxen should have half their usual fare,
Your man, however, should have more: the nights

Are echoing and long. Take care to do
All this until the year comes to an end
And days are equal to the nights, and Earth,
Mother of all, brings forth her various fruits.

When sixty days of winter have gone by
After the solstice, then Arcturus leaves
The holy stream of Ocean,[19] blazing forth
First in the twilight. After him appears·
To men Pandion's high-voiced, mournful child,
The swallow, when the spring has just begun.
You'd better prune your vines before she comes.
But when the One whose house is on his back[20]
Climbs up the stems to flee the Pleiades,
Stop digging vineyards, sharpen your sickles, rouse
Your slaves, and stay away from shady nooks
And sleeping late, till dawn, at harvest time
When the sun burns the skin. Then hurry up
And rising early, gather in your fruits;
Secure your food supply, for Dawn will cut
Your labour by a third; Dawn who assists
You travelling and working, Dawn who shows
The road to men, and helps at yoking-time.

But when the thistle blooms and on the tree
The loud cicada sits and pours his song
Shrill and continuous, beneath his wings,
Exhausting summertime has come. The goats
Are very fat, and wine is very good.
Women are full of lust, but men are weak,
Their heads and limbs drained dry by Sirius,
Their skin parched from the heat. But at this time,
I love a shady rock, and Bibline wine,
A cake of cheese, and goat's milk, and some meat
Of heifers pastured in the woods, uncalved,
Or first-born kids. Then may I sit in shade
And drink the shining wine, and eat my fill

77

And turn my face to meet the fresh West Wind,
And pour three times an offering from the spring
Which always flows, unmuddied, streaming down,
And make my fourth libation one of wine.

When great Orion rises,[21] set your slaves
To winnowing Demeter's holy grain
Upon the windy, well-worn threshing floor.
Then store it, measured, in the jars; when all
Your year's supplies are stowed away, indoors,
Let go the hired man; hire a childless girl
(The ones with nursing infants are no good).
Your sharp-toothed dog should be well cared for, too,
And feed him well, or He Who Sleeps by Day[22]
Will one day snatch away your property.
See to your oxen and your mules, bring in
Sufficient hay, and litter for their stalls;
Then give your slaves a rest; unyoke your team.
But when Orion and the Dog Star move
Into the mid-sky,[23] and Arcturus sees
The rosy-fingered Dawn, then Perses, pluck
The clustered grapes, and bring your harvest home.
Expose them to the sun ten days and nights
Then shadow them for five, and on the sixth
Pour into jars glad Dionysus' gift.
But when the Pleiades and Hyades[24]
And great Orion sink, the time has come
To plough; and fittingly, the old year dies.

But if your heart is captured by desire
For stormy seamanship, this time is worst;
Gales of all winds rage when the Pleiades,
Pursued by violent Orion, plunge
Into the clouded sea. Then keep your ships
No longer on the wine-bright sea, but stay
And work the land, as I have counselled you.
Protect your ship on land with close-packed stones

To shield it from the mighty winds' wet blast;
Unplug the bilge, to keep Zeus and his rain
From rotting it, and then stow all your gear
And tackle in the house, and carefully
Fold up the wings of the sea-going ship,
And hang the well-made rudder over smoke.
Yourself, wait till the sailing season comes,
Then drag your fast ship to the sea and get
A cargo suited to it, which might bring
A profit home, just as our father did,
O foolish Perses, sailing in a ship
Because he longed for great prosperity.
Once, long ago, he crossed far overseas
In his black ship, and came here, to this place,
And left Aeolian Cyme far behind;
He did not flee from riches or success
But evil poverty, which comes from Zeus.
He settled in a wretched village, near
To Helicon, the town of Askra, harsh
In winter, miserable in summertime,
Not really good at any time of year.

But, Perses, keep in mind that all works have
Their proper seasons: sailing, most of all.
Admire small ships, but put your cargo in
A big one, for a larger cargo brings
A larger profit, if the storms hold off.

If you should turn your foolish mind to trade,
Longing to flee from debts and painful want,
I'll teach the measures of the sounding sea,
Unlearned though I am in sea-faring
And ships. For I have sailed upon the sea
Just to Euboea, once, from Aulis, where
There gathered the Achaians, long ago,
From holy Hellas, waiting out the storm,
So they might sail with many men to Troy,

79

Land of fair women. As for me, I crossed
To Chalcis, to wise Amphidamas' games:
The great-souled hero's children had arranged
For many contests, advertised abroad.
And there, I say, I conquered with a song
And carried home a two-eared tripod, which
I set up for the Muses, in that place
On Helicon, the place where I embarked
On lovely singing, first, at their command.
And such is my experience of ships
With all their nails, but even so, I can
Tell you the will of aegis-bearing Zeus,
For I have inspiration in my songs,
Because the Muses taught me how to sing.

The time for men to sail is fifty days[25]
After the solstice, when the exhausting heat
Of summertime is over. Then your ship
Will not be shattered nor your sailors lost
At sea, unless the Shaker of the Earth
Poseidon sets his mind, or Zeus the king
Of the immortals wishes to destroy:
For good results and bad are in their hands.
At this time winds are steady, and the sea
Untroublesome; so trust the winds, and drag
Your swift ship to the sea with confidence;
Load all your cargo in; make haste to sail
And come back home as soon as possible.
Don't wait for the new wine, the autumn rain,
Oncoming storms and Notos' awful blasts;
He stirs the waves, and with him comes much rain
From Zeus at fruit time, and the sea is rough.

Men sail in springtime, also; when a man
Can first see leaves upon the very tops
Of fig-trees, tiny as the prints the crow
Makes with her foot, the sea is passable.

This is spring sailing-time, but as for me,
I will not praise it, and it does not please
My heart: I think this sailing-time is seized
Too hastily, and you might find it hard
To get away from trouble. Men do this
Unwisely, wretched men, for whom the breath
Of life is money. Yet, to die at sea
Among the waves is terrible. But think,
I ask, consider what I say: Do not
Put all your fortune into hollow ships,
Leave most of it behind, and load on board
A smaller share, for it is terrible
To meet catastrophe among the waves
At sea, and terrible to load too great
A weight upon your wagon, and to break
An axle, and have all your cargo lost.
Preserve a sense of right proportion, for
Fitness is all-important, in all things.

Bring home a wife when you are ripe for it;
When you are thirty, not much more nor less,
That is the proper age for marrying.
Your wife should have matured four years before,
And marry in the fifth year. She should be
A virgin; you must teach her sober ways.
Particularly good is one who lives
Nearby, but look around you carefully,
Lest all the neighbours chuckle at your choice.
No prize is better than a worthy wife;
A bad one makes you shiver with the cold;
The greedy wife will roast her man alive[26]
Without the aid of fire, and though he is
Quite tough, she'll bring him to a raw old age.

Beware of angering the blessed gods:
Your friend should not be treated just the same
As you would treat your brother; nonetheless,

If you have such a friend, you must not be
The one to start a quarrel, nor to lie
For the sake of talk; but if he wrongs you first,
With some disloyal word or act, you must
Be sure to pay him double for the wrong.
But if he wants to be your friend again
And says he'll recompense you, take him back;
A man who goes from friend to friend is vile,
But let your mind be open as your face.

Don't be called too hospitable, nor yet
Unfriendly; don't be talked of as too fond
Of lower-class companions, or as one
Who likes to pick a fight with noblemen.

Never reproach a man for poverty
Which eats the heart out and destroys, for it
Is given by the blessed, deathless gods.
A man's best treasure is a thrifty tongue,
His most appealing gift, a tongue that moves
With moderation; for if you should speak
Slander, you'll soon hear worse about yourself.

Do not be rude at crowded common feasts
Where all the guests contribute, for the cost
Is little, and the pleasure very great.

Never omit to wash your hands before
You pour to Zeus and to the other gods
The morning offering of sparkling wine;
They will not hear your prayers, but spit them back.

Do not make water, standing toward the Sun[27]
Unless he has not risen, or has set;
And when you travel, do not urinate
Upon the road or near it; and do not
Expose your body, for the night belongs

82

To the blessed gods. A man who's reverent
And knows much wisdom, sits or goes beside
A courtyard wall, where he will not be seen.

Do not lie down beside the fire when you
Have just made love, and show your naked parts.
Also, it is unwise to sow your seed
When you have just come from a funeral;
Far more auspiciously, beget your child
After a feast of the immortal gods.

Never pass through, on foot, a lovely brook
Of ever-flowing water, till you pray
And look into the beauty of the stream,
And in her clean, sweet water, wash your hands.
For if you cross a river with your hands
And crimes uncleansed, the gods will punish you,
And bring you countless pain in future times.

At the gods' abundant feast, do not cut off[28]
With shining iron, from the five-branched plant,
The dried-up shoots from those which still grow live.

Never, when drinking, leave the ladle in
The mixing-bowl; that brings a fatal jinx.

Don't leave a house half-built, for then a crow
Croaking, might sit on it, and caw bad luck.

A pot unblessed by sacrifice brings harm;
Don't ever eat or wash from such a pot.

Don't let a boy of twelve years, or twelve months,
Sit on a tomb or other sacred thing;
It will unman the baby, or the boy.
Nor should a man use water for his bath
With which a woman bathed herself before;
The punishment is awful, for a time.

If you should come upon a sacrifice
Still burning, do not scoff at things unknown;
This too enrages god. Don't urinate
In springs, or in the mouths of streams which flow
Seaward. This is important to avoid,
And, please, do not relieve yourself in them.[29]

Follow all this; avoid men's gossip, which
Is wicked. Gossip is not hard to raise;
Then, she is light, but burdensome to bear
And hard to unload, when you must carry her.
Gossip is hard to kill when many men
Support her; she is rather like a god.

Observe the days which come from Zeus; [30] instruct
Your slaves to honour them appropriately.
The thirtieth of every month is best
To deal out food and oversee the work.
Men who have judgement know the truth of this:
These days are sent by Zeus the Counsellor.
The following are holy days: the first,
The fourth, the seventh (Leto, on that day,
Brought forth Apollo of the golden sword).
The eight and ninth, of the waxing month, are good
For men to do their work, and very fine
Are the eleventh and the twelfth; those days
Are good for shearing sheep and picking fruit.
But more outstanding is the twelfth, for then
The spider floats on air and spins her web
In daylight, and the Knowing One [31] collects
Her stores. Upon that day a woman should
Set up her loom, and push her work ahead

Avoid the thirteenth of the waxing month
For sowing; it is best for setting plants.

Plants do not prosper on the midmonth sixth,
But it's a lucky birthday for a male,

Unfavourable for girls, either for birth
Or marriage. Again, the first sixth of the month
Is not auspicious for the birth of girls,
But favourable for gelding kids and sheep,
And building sheepfolds, and for bearing boys;
But such a boy will cherish stinging words
And lies, and flattery, and secret talk.
Geld boars and bawling bulls upon the eighth;
The twelfth is better for the labouring mules.
In full day on the twentieth, wise men
Are born, with great intelligence of mind.
The tenth is excellent for bearing males;
The midmonth fourth for females. On that day
Sheep may be trained to bear the touch of hands,
And shuffling oxen and the sharp-toothed dogs
And labouring mules. But in the waxing month
And in the waning, on the fourth, beware
Of heart-consuming worries. On the fourth
Bring home a bride, but let the omens be
Most favourable for marrying that day.

Fifth days are harsh and frightening; take care.
They say that on a fifth, the Furies helped
Strife to bring forth dread Horkos, whom she bore
To bring a punishment to perjurers.

The midmonth seventh is the day to cast
Demeter's holy grain, most carefully,
Out on the well-worn threshing-floor, and let
The carpenter cut lumber for a house
And all the wood that's needed for a ship;
Start building narrow ships upon the fourth.

The midmonth ninth improves toward evening, but
The first ninth is a wholly painless day,
Good to beget both sons and daughters, good
To be born for both, and never wholly bad.

The twenty-seventh [32] of the month is best,
As few men know, for opening a cask
Or putting yokes on oxen or on mules
Or speedy horses, or to haul swift ships
With many benches, to the wine-bright sea.
And few address this day by her right name.

Broach casks upon the fourth; a holy day
Above all others is the midmonth fourth.
Again, few know the twenty-first is best
At dawn, and worsens toward the evening time.

These days are blessings to the men on earth;
The rest are fickle, bland, and bring no luck.
Everyone has his favourite days, but few
Have knowledge that is sure. Sometimes a day
Will be a stepmother, and then she'll change
And be a mother. He is truly blest
And rich who knows these things and does his work,
Guiltless before the gods, and scrupulous,
Observing omens and avoiding wrong.

THEOGNIS

Introduction

THERE are almost no facts about Theognis. His dates, his home city, the details of his life, and the authenticity of many of his poems are matters of scholarly controversy. External evidence (from other ancient writers) is inconsistent and puzzling: for example, some say the poet came from the Megara in Greece, while some insist it was the Sicilian Megara. Internal evidence (drawn from the poems themselves) is even more self-contradictory, confusing and unreliable. On the question of dates, for example: an ancient lexicon, the *Suda*, tells us that Theognis was in his prime about 550 B.C. But one poem curses the Cypselids, whose dynasty in Corinth had ended for ever by about 580; another refers to the Persian invasion, so cannot have been written much before 490. Thus we might conclude that Theognis wrote poems over a period of about ninety years, but none of us can feel really comfortable about that conclusion.

Nevertheless, I will attempt to summarize the main points that seem clear or are fairly generally agreed upon: Theognis lived and wrote chiefly in the sixth century B.C. He came from Megara, probably the one on the Greek mainland, and was an aristocrat. There was a popular revolution, in which he lost his status and probably his money. He seems to have been exiled, and perhaps moved to the Megara in Sicily. He had a young friend named Kurnos, the son of Polypaos, an aristocrat like himself, to whom he wrote numerous poems, mostly consisting of advice about ethics and practical problems. He also wrote elegies to his own soul, to Zeus, to the general public, and perhaps to a number of boys with whom he was intimate (ll. 1231–1388).

His poems were gathered by himself or others into several collections, which duplicate each other to some extent A few poems by other authors (notably Solon, Mimnermus, and Euenos) appear in these collections; we do not know who put them there or why, but generally they fit rather well into the context in which they appear. The various collections of Theognis seem to have been used for various purposes: (1) as texts for Greek children learning to read (they are generally 'improving', and the language is easy and straightforward, but I wonder what sort of education for democracy they provided Athenian boys); (2) as collections of drinking songs for use at symposia; and (3) as political propaganda for the aristocratic point of view, perhaps circulated *sub rosa* by members of the oligarchic clubs in Athens. Somewhere, at some point, someone put together several of these collections, and added a collection of inoffensive homosexual poems, many of them perhaps by Theognis (ll. 1231–1388), and made the collection of collections which we have today. For what purpose?

Purely as literature, I would guess: the collection as we have it now would never do as a school text, or a collection of drinking lyrics, or a political treatise: it is too self-contradictory for political use, too serious for symposium use, too grown-up for school use. It is not a didactic work, although many of the elegies in it are themselves didactic; it is an anthology to be read for pleasure, which displays the many moods and themes of a fine poet, ranging from serious theological questioning to playful riddles to intensely personal love lyrics. Theognis is historically interesting, of course. He displays the political views of a typical sixth-century aristocrat. He shows us an important stage in Greek religious thought, in which the justice of Zeus was being seriously questioned. He presents to us the distress and confusion of those who live in an age of transition from one set of values (based on agrarian, hereditary nobility) to another (based on money and the city). He shows us much about the rather rigid behaviour patterns of the upper-class homosexual. His poems provide a wealth of information about everyday ethics and etiquette. But I feel strongly that anyone who reads Theognis only for his historical interest will miss the point which his unknown ancient editor clearly perceived, that Theognis was a poet, 'the Muses' man and messenger', first of all.

The chief virtue of Theognis' poetry at its best is its *strength*. He is a poet of strong opinions, strong emotions and strong words. 'Let me drink their black blood,' he screams of his enemies. 'I will never get so drunk as to say one bad word of you,' he says to a loved one. Rather than be caught by Poverty, he suggests, 'Leap into the monster-filled sea, or from a rocky cliff!' 'Don't goad me; don't try to *drive* my love,' he complains to Kurnos. 'What handsome fees doctors would earn,' he reflects, 'If they could cure badness or a muddled brain.' 'The city's pregnant,' he says, 'And I'm afraid she'll give birth to a violent leader of civil war.'

Metaphor (which Aristotle considered the one unteachable, inborn and central component of poetry) furnishes the chief strength of Theognis' style. For example, he wishes to say that the citizens of his town are excessively swayed by demagogues. How does he express it?

> Stamp on the empty-headed people! Jab
> With your pointed goad, and lay the heavy yoke
> Around their necks! You won't find under the sun
> A people who love slavery so much.   [847–50]

He reproves a young lover for unfaithfulness:

> When I drank alone at that black-watered spring
> The water tasted clean and sweet to me;
> But now it is polluted, mixed with mud,
> I'll go to other sources for my drinks.   [959–62]

For the conventional idea that we should enjoy ourselves while we are young:

> Let's give our hearts to banqueting, while we
> Can still find pleasure in delightful things.
> For glorious youth goes by as fast as thought,
> Faster than horses charging recklessly,
> Bringing their master to the work of war
> While they delight in the smooth, wheat-bearing plain.
>   [983–8]

I think there is a particularly good contrast here, between the high-spirited horses enjoying their easy ride – i.e., the thoughtless, happy emotions of youth – and their master who must go to the labour and sorrow of battle – man, the 'master' of his passions, who must face his responsibilities, old age, and ultimate death.

On the importance of eugenics:

> Slave heads don't ever stand up straight; they grow
> Tipped down in servitude, their necks bent low;
> No rose nor hyacinth comes from the wild
> Squill, nor does a slave bear a free child. [535–8]

Although he is a strongly metaphorical poet, he is seldom 'fancy'. He rarely alludes to mythology or requires any special knowledge of his reader; he uses adjectives sparingly; his vocabulary is simple and his word order direct and clear. Although he wrote many variations on a few favourite themes, he is almost never redundant or windy in any one poem; he says what he wants to say, as strongly and economically as he can, and then stops. His tone, like that of Juvenal (the great Roman satirist) is often heavily ironic; for example in this couplet to Ploutos, the god of wealth:

> Hail, Ploutos, finest of gods and most beloved!
> With you a serf becomes a gentleman. [1117–81]

And, like Juvenal, Jonathan Swift, or Mark Twain, in the savagery of his attacks he often raises a laugh. Not a light-hearted laugh, but the hopeless, harsh and almost hysterical laugh that comes with the last straw.

Unfortunately, as his personality is revealed in the poems, Theognis is not at all likeable. He seems to have been a savage, paranoid, bigoted, bitter, narrow, pompous, self-pitying person. Over and over, he reproves Kurnos and various other friends for being unfaithful to him, for deceiving him, for letting him down. The lower classes are 'the bad'; aristocrats are 'the good'. But even among gentlemen, almost everyone is untrustworthy, and few have any brains. It's better never to be born, second best to die young. Nothing ever works out the way you planned it. Good men suffer; bad men thrive. Old age is an unalloyed disaster, and death is vile and frightening. Everyone lacks gratitude; the 'low' are particularly bad in this respect (yet Theognis himself never, in any poem we have, expressed gratitude to anyone for anything). He is often self-contradictory. He is particularly ambivalent about money. On the one hand, he says repeatedly that a good man is brave and patient 'in bad times', and that greed leads to wickedness; he complains with bitter sarcasm that gentlemen nowadays are willing to marry any sort of trash for money; he attacks the lower classes and his friends for caring about nothing else. On the other hand, he calls Poverty a 'slut', a 'jailer', a 'seducer', 'worse than fever or grey Old Age', and 'the mother of impotence', and he never stops lamenting the loss of his money and calling on the gods to help him get it back and get revenge. He is equally inconsistent about the value of consistency. He urges Kurnos to act like the sea-polyp which changes colour to match the rock it's on; in many poems he praises duplicity, flattery of 'low' men, adjusting one's behaviour and opinions to match one's neighbours; but then he attacks the two-faced man, the 'mixing-bowl' friend, he complains how hard it is to know the mind of a man, and he says that the worth of a man must be tested in a crisis, as gold is rubbed by a touchstone, and that only he, Theognis, has ever been found as true and pure as fine gold, tested beside mere lead.

What an impossible person! A major problem about paranoid people is that they attract persecution, and quite possibly this was the case with Theognis. If you call your friends slanderous traitors often enough, sooner or later they will slander and betray you and prove you right. Reading Theognis, one can't help feeling a bit sorry for Kurnos: only his name, really, has been immortalized; the poet neglects to tell us anything about his great love, except that he was unfaithful. We never learn what Kurnos looked like, what made him lovable, what he thought about anything, what he did that was good or brave or amusing or endearing. What kind of love is that?

Still we must remember that Theognis' attitudes were not so

pathological in his culture as they would be in ours. Boasting was considered quite proper by the Greeks, as was crying about one's misfortunes. (Prometheus, the hero of Aeschylus' *Prometheus Bound*, written in the fifth century, does a great deal of both, as does Achilles, the hero of the *Iliad*, written several centuries earlier. In fact most Greek heroes are quite childlike and natural in their responses to success or failure. No Christian modesty for them – also, no humble resignation.) Pessimism about life and the nature of man was standard. (See, for example, Hesiod's description of the Ages of Man, *Works and Days*, 170 ff, pp. 64–5.) Class hatred – the distinction between gentlemen, 'the good', and the working people, 'the bad' – was universal among the aristocrats of the sixth century. The desire for violent revenge was considered not only natural but quite proper, before Socrates. And as for paranoia, let us consider Odysseus, the hero of the *Odyssey*, who embodied intelligence and wisdom for the Greeks of all successive generations. In what did his 'wisdom' consist? Chiefly, in suspiciousness – he never told his right name or gave anyone a straight answer. He was cautious, always expecting the worst of everyone. In fact, paranoia *was* intelligence, in a world full of cannibals, pirates, monsters, treacherous suitors, and untrustworthy gods. And for Theognis, living in a time of social change, civil war and reversal of values, the city of Megara must have seemed as dangerous, uncertain and wild as the strange world of Odysseus' sea voyages; both were risky worlds full of real persecution.

So we can forgive Theognis – a little – for his savage and suspicious nature. And the absolution will be complete, I trust, when we reflect that it is his least appealing personal qualities – his bitterness, his self-pity and his vengefulness – which give the better elegies most of their extraordinary power.

All the poems of Theognis are in the elegiac metre, which was normally accompanied by the flute. Elegiac couplets were considered by the Greeks to be appropriate for many themes: love, laments for the dead, scurrilous personal abuse, philosophical observations, political propaganda, and riddles. The metre is basically dactylic; the first line of the couplet is hexameter, the second pentameter. It is an unnatural metre for English, so I have done my translation mostly in blank verse (unrhymed iambic pentameter, the most natural English metre), although I have occasionally used a different metre or allowed some rhymes to intrude, where I felt it would be appropriate, to present a particularly noteworthy poem. I am more colloquial in my translations of Theognis than I am with Hesiod: there is a difference of tone in the authors.

Bibliography

I have based my translation on the Greek text of Jean Carrière (Budé edition, Paris, 1962), compared with those of J. M. Edmonds (Loeb Library, 1958) and D. Young (Teubner, 1961). In textual doubt, I have allowed two out of the three to sway me; if all three disagreed I have made my own decision, but have generally found Carrière's text the most translatable, and his commentary extremely helpful. I have followed Edmond's line numbering throughout.

There is very little for the general reader which is in English and in print. The best discussion I know of is in C. M. Bowra, *Early Greek Elegists* (Oxford, 1938), pages 139-70.

Note on the text of Theognis

Some of these poems are better than others. As Martial said, you can't make a book any other way. I have marked the ones I like best with a *.

Those poems which I am quite sure were not written by Theognis I have marked with a † in the margin. When the real author is known, I give him credit in a footnote.

Prose translations of several important poems also appear in the footnotes. These are poems which I handled rather freely in my verse translation.

Theognis, *Elegies*

† O LORD, the son of Leto, child of Zeus,[1]
I won't forget you now or at the end.
I'll sing you first and last and in between,
You, listen, and be favourable to me.   [1-4]

*† When lady Leto, Phoebus, at your birth,
Holding the slender palm-tree, gripped it tightly
Near by the Delian lake – for you, fair child,
Celestial perfume filled the district; Earth
Shook her huge frame with laughter; brightly
The face of white-haired Ocean gleamed and smiled.   [5-10]

† O huntress Artemis, daughter of Zeus,
Honoured by Agamemnon when he sailed
To Troy in his fast ships, please hear my prayer:
Keep off the evil spirits; no hard task
For you, a goddess, but great for me, a man.   [11-14]

† Muses and Graces, daughters of Zeus, who came
To Cadmus' wedding, once, you sang these words:
'The beautiful is good, and if a thing's
Not beautiful, it isn't good.' This was
The song that came from your immortal lips.   [15-18]

* I seal my words of wisdom with your name,[2]
Kurnos; no man can steal them now, nor try
To slip his trash in with my excellence,
And every man will say, 'This is a song
That great Theognis, the Megarian, sang.'

I don't please all the men of Megara;
So what: not even Zeus is praised by all,
Whether he holds his rain or lets it fall.   [19-26]

* These things I tell you, Kurnos, for your good:
I learned them, as a boy, from gentlemen;
Rule one: no honour, prize, or cash reward
Can justify a base or crooked act.
The second rule: avoid 'low' company,
Mix only with the better sort of men.
Drink with these men, and eat, and sit with them,
And court them, for their power is great; from them
You will learn goodness. Men of little worth
Will spoil the natural virtue of your birth.
Do this and you'll acknowledge, in the end,
Theognis gave good counsel to his friend.   [27-38]

* This city's pregnant, Kurnos, and I fear
She'll bear a man to crush our swelling pride.
The people still have sense, but those in charge
Are turning, stumbling into evil ways.   [39-42]

* Gentlemen never yet destroyed a town;
But when the scum resort to violence,
Seduce the masses and corrupt the courts
To line their pockets and increase their power,
Then, Kurnos, you may know this tranquil town
Cannot remain unshaken very long.
When wicked men rejoice in private graft
Then public evils follow; factions rise,
Then bloody civil war, until the state
Welcomes a Tsar. God save us from that fate!   [43-52]

* Kurnos, the city stands; her men are changed.
You know, in former days, there was a tribe
Who knew no laws nor manners, but like deer
They grazed outside the city walls, and wore

The skins of goats. These men are nobles, now.
The gentlemen of old are now the trash;
Terrible sight. No principles at all:
These new men cheat each other, and they *laugh*.
Don't give your heart to any of these men,
Whatever profit seems to lie in it.
Pretend, my Kurnos, that you love them all,
But when it comes to something serious,
Stay clear; for in their pitiable hearts
You'll find no honour, and their love, you'll learn,
Is all for mischief, for a cruel joke;
Their faith, like that of souls already doomed.   [53–68]

In business matters, Kurnos, never give
Your wholesale trust to an immoral man;
Go to a man of honour with your plans,
If it means walking many miles on foot.   [69–72]

Don't even share your thoughts with all your friends;
Of all their number, few deserve your trust.   [73–4]

To save yourself much pain: the bigger your plans
The smaller the group of friends should share in them.   [75–6]

Kurnos, in troubled times a faithful man
Is worth his weight in silver, and in gold.   [77–8]

* Polypaides, few of those friends of yours
Will still be friends of yours if hard times come.
And blessed few have guts enough to share
Your poverty as now they share your wealth.   [79–82]

* Ransack mankind, my friend, and find all those
With honour – the sense of shame [3] – still in their eyes
And on their tongues, who never could be bought
For any price: one boat would hold the lot.   [83–6]

* Oh, Kurnos, if you love me as you say,
  Don't cuddle up with words and let your mind
  Go wandering elsewhere; either keep your thoughts
  Wholly for me, or tell me now, straight out,
  You hate me; quarrel, and let the break be clean.
  A friend who lies so well is frightening;
  I'd rather have you for an enemy.   [87–92]

* A friend who compliments you to your face
  And runs you down in other company,
  Who speaks fair words, but thinks the opposite,
  Is not a friend one really wants to have.
  Give me a man who understands my moods,
  Who, brother-like, bears with my grouchiness.
  If you will give your mind to what I say,
  Dear friend, you will remember me, one day.   [93–100]

  Don't ever choose a rascal for a friend,
  Kurnos. What use is friendship with the low?
  If you're in trouble, failing, he won't help
  And if he prospers, he won't share with you.   [101–104]

* Only a fool does favours for the base;
  You'd do as well to sow the grey salt sea.
  No crop of corn would come up from the deep,
  No gratitude, no favours from the base.
  The scum are never sated. If you slip,
  Just once, their former friendship melts away.
  But put a gentleman once in your debt,
  You have a friend for life; he won't forget.   [105–12]

  Never bestow your friendship on a rascal,
  He is a harbour full of rocks; avoid him.   [113–14]

  For drinking comrades, many men will do;
  For more important business, precious few.
  To spot a man who's counterfeit is hard,
  But nothing, Kurnos, matters quite so much.   [115–18]

Smart men aren't often fooled by phony coins
And when they are, the loss is bearable;
But, Kurnos, when a man deceives his friend
And carries in his breast a cunning heart,
That is the basest thing that God has made,
The hardest counterfeit to recognize.
The mind of man or woman can't be known
Until it's seen in harness, like a horse;
You cannot guess the value of the goods
By close examination: looks deceive.   [119–28]

Don't pray for outstanding wealth or excellence,
Kurnos; the one great thing for man is Luck.   [129–30]

Kurnos, there's nothing better for a man
Than parents who love and keep the holy law.   [131–32]

No mortal, Kurnos, makes his own success,
Nor his own ruin, for the gods bring both.
Nor is there any man who knows at heart
If in the end he works for good or bad.
Often he thinks he'll fail, and then he wins,
Often expects to win – and then he fails.
No one gets all he wants; all men stop short,
Checked by the boundaries of the possible.
We think our thoughts in vain, all ignorant,
The gods do everything just as they want.   [133–42]

Kurnos, no man who harms a suppliant
Or wrongs a guest can ever fool the gods.   [143–4]

It's better, Kurnos, to be poor and good
Than rich and crooked, if you have to choose.
All excellence amounts to being just,
And all real gentlemen obey the rules.   [145–8]

Even to worthless men the gods give wealth,
Kurnos – but excellence they give to few.   [149–50]

The first thing, Kurnos, which the gods bestow
On one they would annihilate, is pride.   [151-2]

† Excess engenders pride, when money falls
To men with minds unfitted for its use.⁴   [153-4]

Never, in anger, castigate a man
For poverty, which wastes and kills the heart.
Zeus tilts his balance this way and then that,
One moment you're a rich man, next you're not.   [155-8]

Don't talk too big in public, Kurnos; who
Knows what the coming night or day will bring?   [159-60]

Many a stupid man has striking luck
And turns apparent failure to success;
Many a brilliant man, whose luck is bad,
Labours through all his life for no reward.   [161-4]

No man is rich or poor, or good or bad
Unless his private daimon⁵ makes him so.   [165-6]

Each man on earth has his own sorry fate
The sun sees no one truly fortunate.   [167-8]

The lucky man is honoured by the gods
And by his critics with their envious blame,
But earnest striving wins no praise at all.   [169-70]

Pray to the gods, the gods have all the power.
All good and evil come to men from them.   [171-2]

* Fever and grey Old Age subdue good men;
But nothing, Kurnos, masters a gentleman
More damnably than Poverty. To get
Away from her, jump in the monstrous sea
Or from a rocky cliff! The man who has
Poverty for a jailer cannot speak
Or act as he would wish; his tongue is chained.   [173-8]

On land, Kurnos, and on the sea's broad back
Hunt for release from wretched Poverty.   [179–80]

Better Kurnos, for a poor man to die
Than live rubbed raw by wretched Poverty.   [181–2]

* You want to buy an ass? a horse?
You'll pick a thoroughbred, of course,
For quality is in the blood.
But when a *man* goes out to stud –
He won't refuse a commoner
If lots of money goes with her.
And vulgar oafs with brutish ways
Can marry noble girls, these days.
Good faith means nothing now, it's clear,
Hard cash is all that's honoured here,
While gentle blood unites with base –
The drachma's ruining our race.
You wonder, lad, that I disparage
The present state of civil marriage?[6]   [183–92]

Seduced by money, a gentleman will take
A bride he knows is trash, and lead her home,
Although he has a fine old name and she
No name at all; for strong Necessity
Urges him on, Necessity, which makes
Men capable of standing anything.   [193–6]

Possessions that come from Zeus, and follow just
And clean behaviour, always last secure.
But if a greedy man improperly
Acquires them by some crime or lying oath,
At first he seems to profit, but at last
He ends in sorrow; the gods' will prevails.
This is what fools men's minds: the Blessed Ones
Do not repay offences instantly.
One man, who pays himself his evil debt,

Leaves no doom hanging over his dear sons,
Another is not caught by Justice, or
Too soon his eyes are closed by shameless Death.　　[197-208]

An exile has no fond or loyal friend,
And this is worse than exile is, itself.　　[209-10]

To drink too much is bad: but if you would
Drink wisely, you'd find wine not bad, but good.　　[211-12]

* My soul: be changeable with all your friends,
Adapt yourself to each one's mood and style.
See how the clinging polyp, for protection,
Matches his colour to the cliff's complexion;
The subtle creature thus escapes detection.
For each new situation, change your style,
Adjust your patter, modify your smile:
Consistency's inferior to guile.7　　[213-18]

When the city is upset, Kurnos, keep calm.
And stay, as I do, on the middle road.　　[219-20]

Whoever thinks his neighbour does not know
Anything, and that he himself alone
Plans subtly, is a fool and his good brain
Is sick. We all can think of crafty plans,
But this man will not stoop to crookedness,
While that one loves duplicity and guile.　　[221-6]

† No end to money-making's set for men:
For those who have the most work twice as hard
For more. And who could satisfy them all?
The quest for goods turns into craziness,
And ruin follows, falling first on one,
Then on another sufferer, sent by Zeus.8　　[227-32]

A man who is acropolis and tower
To an empty-headed crowd wins little fame
Or honour, Kurnos, for his excellence.   [233-4]

We must not act as men who have escaped
Disaster, Kurnos, but as men who know
Their city certainly will be destroyed.[9]   [235-6]

* I give you wings. You'll soon be lifted up
Across the land, across the boundless crests
Of ocean; where men dine and pass the cup,
You'll light there, on the lips of all the guests,
Where lithe, appealing lads will praise you, swelling
Their song to match the piper's sweet, shrill tone.
At length, my boy, you'll enter Hades' dwelling,
That black hole where departed spirits moan,
But even then your glory will not cease,
Your well-loved name will stay alive, unworn;
You'll skim across the mainland, over Greece,
Over the islands and the sea, not borne
By horses, Kurnos; you'll be whirled along
By violet-crowned maids, the Muses; yours
Will be each practised singer's finest song,
As long as light exists and earth endures.
I give you this, for what? To be reviled –
To be betrayed and lied to, like a child.[10]   [237-54]

The loveliest thing is justice, and the best
Is health; the happiest thing: to win one's love.   [255-6]

I am a champion mare and beautiful.
I carry a bad man. This brings me pain
And often I have almost burst the reins
And thrown my evil rider, and escaped.[11]   [257-60]

* I do not serve the wine to that sweet girl;
Another (no match for me) does that, while I

Serve fresh cold water to her parents. Still,
She often takes me to the well and then
Supports me, groaning; while I kiss her neck
With arms around her, and she sweetly moans.[12]   [261-6]

We all know Poverty; even when she
Is someone else's mistress. We will not
Allow her in the public square or courts;
She gets inferior treatment everywhere
And everywhere is muttered at and loathed.   [267-70]

Men get a fair share, from the gods, of youth
And horrid age and many another thing.
But one thing's worst of all, more terrible
Than death or any sickness: when you raise
Children and give them all the tools of life,
And suffer greatly getting wealth for them,
And then they hate their father, pray he'll die
And loathe him as a beggar in their midst.   [271-8]

It seems the bad man doesn't understand
The ways of Justice, for he has no fear
Of Nemesis to come. For a base man
The easiest way's to snatch what's close at hand
And to imagine all will turn out well.   [279-82]

Among these citizens don't take one step,
Relying on their friendship, or an oath
From one, not if he offers Great King Zeus
As witness, or the gods as sureties.
No one can please a slanderous town like this.
Poor men have little chance of being spared.   [283-8]

Now ways thought bad by good men have become
Excellent ways to these bad men who rule
With novel laws which wander from the road;
The sense of shame has died, and violence
And wrong have conquered right, and rule the world.   [289-92]

The lion does not always dine on meat,
Sometimes, strong as he is, he finds no prey. [293-4]

The heaviest burden for a talky man
Is silence; everywhere he goes he talks
And is a bore, disliked by all. To sit
With him at dinner is like being jailed. [295-8]

Kurnos, no one befriends a luckless man
Not even if one belly bore them both. [299-300]

Be sweet, then bitter, kind, then harsh to slaves,
To servants, and to neighbours at your door. [301-302]

Don't wag the tail of life, if it goes well,
But leave it undisturbed. If it should go
Badly, rock it until it straightens up. [303-304]

The bad did not spring evil from the womb:
Rather, in company with evil men
They learned low ways, vile words, and violence,
And swallowed everything their low friends said. [305-308]

The wise man at a party sees no gaffes;
For him, they never happened. While he dines
He jokes and puts his serious self aside;
Matching his mood to everyone he meets.[13] [309-12]

When men are acting wild, I am most wild;
Among the just, I am most just of all. [313-14]

† Bad men are often rich, and good men poor.
But we would not exchange our virtue for
Their wealth. Our virtue always is secure,
While money goes to this one, then to that.[14] [315-18]

A good man, Kurnos, keeps his character
In bad times and in good; but if the God
Gives money and good life to a bad man
The fool cannot hold back his evilness.   [319-22]

Never, Kurnos, for little cause destroy
A friend because you trust a slanderous lie.   [323-4]

A man who's always angry with his friend
For any fault will have no peace nor friends.
Along with mortals, Kurnos, come mistakes;
Only the gods will not put up with them.   [325-8]

The prudent slow man overtakes the quick
If the gods' justice, Kurnos, runs with him.   [329-30]

Walk calmly as I do, the middle road;
Don't give to this man, Kurnos, that man's goods.   [331-2]

An exile has no fond or loyal friend,
And this is worse than exile is, itself.[15]   [332a-b]

Kurnos, don't put much faith in exiled friends,
When they get home, they're not the men you knew.   [333-4]

Not too much zeal! The middle way is best;
There, Kurnos, you'll find good, so hard to get.   [335-6]

Zeus, let me pay my friends for all their love,
And give me power over my enemies!
Then, Kurnos, I will seem a very god
If I can die with all debts paid in full.   [337-40]

* O Zeus of Olympus, fulfil my just prayer,
For my pains, give me some bit of fortune again,
Or kill me, if nothing will ease my despair,
If I'll get no relief, no revenge on those men.

Only just? But those robbers who swagger around
With my gold – is it Justice that leaves them their gains
Wrenched away in the deluge, while I, wretched hound,
Lost my all in the storm? No possession remains.
Oh, if only some powerful god could be found
For my cause, I would drink the black blood from their veins![16]

[341-50]

* Ah Poverty, you slut! Why do you stay?
Why love me when I hate you? Please betray
Me for another man, and be his wife;
Why must you always share my wretched life? [351-4]

Have courage now in bad times, as you had
Delight when fortune, Kurnos, favoured you;
Your luck was good, then bad; now try to slip
Out of misfortune's garment, with god's help.
But do it in the dark; too much display
Of misery will bring few comforters. [355-60]

A man's heart, Kurnos, shrinks when he receives
Injury; when he's avenged, it grows again. [361-2]

Flatter your enemy; but when you get
The upper hand, without pretext, strike back! [363-4]

Be firm at heart, with honey on your tongue;
Only low men are quick to take offence. [365-6]

* I cannot understand these citizens:
I cannot please them, whether I do good
Or harm. Many, both good and bad men, hate me
But none of these simpletons can imitate me. [367-70]

Kurnos: don't goad me under the yoke against
My will; don't try to drive my love too much. [371-2]

* I am surprised at you, dear Zeus! You're lord
Everywhere, hold all honour and great power;
You know the mind and heart of every man;
Your rule's supreme, my king, in all the world.
How then, O son of Kronos, can your mind
Bear to see criminals and honest men –
Both thoughtful men whose minds are moderate,
And sinful weaklings – share the selfsame fate?
No divine rules are fixed for men, no road
To travel which will surely please the gods.　　　　　[373–82]

The wicked men have carefree wealth, while they
Who keep their hearts from evil, nonetheless
Get poverty, the mother of impotence
For all their love of justice. Poverty
Leads many a man to crime; necessity
Corrupts his thinking and he learns to bear,
Unwillingly, much shame. He yields to want,
The teacher of all evil, cheating, lies,
And deadly quarrels; though the man resists,
Unfitted for wrongdoing, still he yields:
Thus poverty gives birth to impotence.[17]　　　　　[383–92]

In poverty, when want is pressing hard
The base man and his better can be known
For what they are: the just man still is just,
His upright mind unchanged; the other's lost
The power of choosing either good or bad.[18]　　　　　[393–97]

Not too much zeal! Appropriateness is best
In every human act. Often a man
Pursuing wealth is eager to excel;
And all the while his daimon[19] leads him on
Into a great confusion, so he thinks
What's bad is good, and what is useful, bad.　　　　　[401–406]

You made a mistake in being loved too much,
I'm not the cause; it's you who were unwise.　　　　　[407–408]

You cannot leave a treasure to your sons
More precious, Kurnos, than the sense of shame[20]
Which comes as the companion of good men.   [409-10]

No man seems better, Kurnos, for a friend,
Than one who has good sense and also power.   [411-12]

I shall not arm myself with drink so far
Nor let myself be led so far by wine
As to say even one bad word of you.   [413-14]

Searching, I've found no comrade like myself,
A faithful friend, in whom there's no deceit.
Put to the test, like gold beside mere lead,
I will be found superior every time.   [415-18]

I perceive much that passes by, but keep
Silence; I must, knowing my lack of power.   [419-20]

Too many tongues have gates which fly apart
Too easily, and care for many things
That don't concern them. Better to keep bad news
Indoors, and only let the good news out.   [421-4]

For man the best thing is never to be born,
Never to look upon the hot sun's rays,
Next best, to speed at once through Hades' gates
And lie beneath a piled-up heap of earth.   [425-8]

* It's easier to get and raise a child
Than to put character in him. No one
Has ever found a way to make a fool
Wise or a bad man good. If God had taught
This to the children of Asclepius[21] –
How to cure badness or a muddled brain –
What handsome fees they'd earn! And if good sense
Could be man-made and planted in a child,

III

Good fathers, giving sensible advice,
Would never have bad sons. I wish it could,
But teaching cannot make a bad man good.   [429-38]

That man's a fool who keeps a constant watch
Over my thoughts, and quite neglects his own.   [439-40]

No one is always lucky in all things;
Good men endure bad luck without complaint,
The common man cannot control himself
In good times or in bad. All sorts of gifts
Come to us mortals from the gods; we must
Endure, whatever sorts of gifts they give.   [441-6]

Come, wash me: see, the water trickles down
Unstained and pure at all times, from my head.
In all my acts, you'll find me like fine gold,
Rubbed by the touchstone, rosy to look upon,
Whose surface is untarnished and unmarked
By stains, and always keeps its colour pure.   [447-52]

Good sir; if you possessed a brain as big
As your stupidity, or were as wise
As you are stupid now, you'd be admired
By all, as much as you are now despised.   [453-6]

A young wife is no prize for an old man.
She's like a ship whose rudder does not work;
Her anchors never hold. At night she breaks
Her moorings, and drifts to another port.   [457-60]

Don't fix your mind on things that can't be done;
Don't long for that which never will be yours.   [461-2]

The gods don't make us terrible or great
With ease: fame comes to those who work for it.   [463-4]

Spend time on excellence, and love the right,
And don't let shameful profit master you.   [465-6]

†* Don't hold the unwilling guest, Simonides,
But don't expel the friend who wants to stay.
Don't rouse your drunken comrade whom sweet sleep
Has caught, but let the wakeful stay awake:
All force is disagreeable. Stand by
Ready to pour for those who want to drink:
We cannot have a party every night.
Still, because I am moderate in my use
Of honeyed wine, I reach my house before
I think of soothing sleep, and I make clear
How fine a beverage for man is wine:
I'm no teetotaller, but not a lush.
The man who drinks too much cannot control
His tongue or mind; he rambles foolishly
Embarrassing his sober friends. He's not
Ashamed of his behaviour when he's drunk.
Even though he was sensible before,
Now, he's an ass. But you, who know all this,
Don't overdo your drinking: quietly
Get up and go before you're drunk, or if
You'd stay, then have no more to drink – don't let
Your belly master you, as if you were
A common labourer. That stupid word
'Pour!' which you're always babbling, has made
Your drunkenness. First, you drink to a friend,
Then, for a bet; another's for the gods;
The next, because – it's in your hand, you can't
Say no. The winner of a drinking bout
Really is one who drinks and still does not
Talk stupidly. All you who stay beside
The mixing-bowl: try to converse as well
As possible; let no hostility
Intrude; let your remarks be general,
And you will have a fine symposium.[22]   [467-96]

Wine makes the wise man level with the fool:
The drunkard's mind becomes as light as air. [497-8]

Experts test gold and silver in the fire;
Wine is the test to show the mind of man;
Even a wise man, clever up till now,
When he gets drunk, brings shame upon himself. [499-502]

* My head is heavy, Onomacritus, –
Wine pushes me, – I'm not the manager
Of what I think – the room is running round.
Let me get up and find out if the wine
Controls my feet the way it does my head –
I'm scared that I'll do something asinine
And shame myself, I'm so far gone with wine. [503-508]

To drink too much is bad, but if you would
Drink wisely, you'd find wine not bad, but good.[23] [509-10]

You've crossed the sea and come, without a cent,
Poor Clearistus, to a penniless host.
I'll share what I've been given by the gods;
We'll stow it in your ship, next to the ribs
Under the rowing benches. I will give
Unstintingly of all the best I have;
But even for your friendship I'll not go
To borrow elsewhere. If a friend of yours
Arrives, – truly a friend – he may sleep here.
And if you're asked how well I'm doing, say:
'Not badly, for a poor man. For a rich,
Badly indeed. He wouldn't turn away
His father's friend, but more he can't support.' [511-22]

* Ploutos, no wonder mortals worship you:[24]
You are so tolerant of all their sins! [523-4]

It would be fair if good men had the wealth
And poverty fell to the evil men. [525-6]

* Damn youth; damn miserable age! The one
For coming, and the other, for leaving me. [527-8]

I never have betrayed a friend or true
Comrade; there is no slavery in my soul. [529-30]

My heart grows warm inside, each time I hear
The lovely voices of the singing flutes. [531-2]

It makes me happy to drink well, and sing
To flutes, and take in hand the sweet-voiced lyre. [533-4]

* Slave heads don't ever stand up straight, they grow
Tipped down in servitude, their necks bent low;
No rose or hyacinth comes from the wild
Squill, nor does a slave bear a free child. [535-8]

Kurnos, unless the gods deceive my mind,
That man is forging fetters for himself. [539-40]

Kurnos, I fear that pride's destroyed this town
As it did the Centaurs, eaters of raw flesh. [541-2]

I have to judge this case with rule and square,
Kurnos, and give fair hearing to each side,
Make use of prophets, birds, burnt offerings,
To spare myself the shame of a mistake. [543-6]

Don't force your way by badness; for the just,
Nothing succeeds so well as doing good. [547-8]

* Kurnos, a voiceless messenger, which shines [25]
From the watching-place, far-seeing, rouses us
To a war of many tears. Put bridles on
The swift-heeled horses, for I think they must
Face enemies. Not far away they'll find
These men, unless the gods deceive my mind. [549-54]

The man who lies in sore pain must be brave
And ask the deathless gods for his release.   [555-6]

Beware: you're standing on the razor's edge;
One way, you're rich; the other way you're poor;
Try not to fall into excessive wealth,
Nor yet to slide into great poverty.   [557-60]

I'd like to get my enemies' property,
Some for myself, and much for all my friends.   [561-2]

It's good to be invited to a feast
And sit beside a gentleman who knows
What wisdom is. Listen when he speaks truth,
And take his wisdom home with you, pure gain.   [563-6]

I play, enjoying youth. For I will lie
A long time underground, when life is gone,
Mute as a stone, and leave the sun's dear light;
Fine though I was, I shall see nothing more.   [567-70]

Reputation's an evil, trial is best.
Many have good repute that are untried.   [571-2]

Do good and you'll receive it. Why send out
Announcements? News of good work travels fast.   [573-4]

* The pilot steers around the rocks at sea,
Just so, I can avoid my enemy;
It is my friends who are the death of me.   [575-6]

Good becomes bad more easily than bad
Turns good. Don't teach me; I'm too old to learn.   [577-8]

I hate a bad man and I go disguised
With the airy spirit of a little bird.[26]   [579-80]

I hate a wife who runs around; I hate
Also the rogue who ploughs another's field.   [581-2]

The past is finished, and can't be undone,
Care for the future should be our concern.   [583-4]

† There's risk in everything, and no one knows
When he conceives a plan, where it will lead.
One man who's bent on reputation falls
Through lack of foresight into frightful doom,
Another, doing good, is given by God
Good sense and happy fortune in all things.[27]   [585-90]

Men must endure whatever the gods give
And lightly bear our share of good and bad,
In bad times not too sick at heart; in good,
Not glad too soon, before we see the end.   [591-4]

My friend, let's be companions from afar;
One tires of everything (except of wealth).
Let's still be friends; but you, take up with men
Who understand you better than I do.   [595-8]

* You haven't fooled me, travelling that road
Where you have ridden formerly, and spoiled
Our friendship. Go to hell, you enemy
Of gods, traitor to men, you slippery snake[28]
Whose chill I held and warmed within my breast!   [599-602]

Magnesia was destroyed by pride and crimes
Like those now rampant in this holy town.   [603-604]

Plenty's destroyed more men than famine's killed,
People who wanted more than was their due.   [605-606]

At first, a lie may bring a little gain;
Then that gain turns to evil and to shame;
Once past the lips, the lie brings nothing good,
But dogs the liar everywhere he goes.   [607-610]

It's easy to blame your neighbour and to praise
Yourself; the masses do a lot of this;
Gossiping, slandering, they won't shut up
But gentlemen keep measure in all things.   [611-14]

The sun looks on no man of nowadays
Who is entirely good and moderate.   [615-16]

Men do not often get their heart's desire:
Gods are more powerful than mortal man.[29]   [617-18]

I toss about in problems, anxiously:
I've yet to sail around Cape Poverty.   [619-20]

The sentiments of all men are the same,
They all love rich men, and despise the poor.   [621-2]

All sorts of evils are in mortal men
All sorts of virtues, too, and ways of life.   [623-4]

It's painful for a wise man to speak out
In company with fools; and yet to be
At all times, silent – that's impossible.   [625-6]

Among sober men, a drunk's embarrassing;
Likewise a sober man among the drunks.   [627-8]

Youth and naiveté cause silliness
Which often gets a boy into a fix.   [629-30]

Kurnos, the man whose head does not control
His heart, is always landing in disgrace
And spends his life in great perplexity.   [631-2]

If a good idea pops into your head
Reflect on it again, and then again:
The rash are always ruined in the end.   [633-4]

Honour and sense go with the gentleman;
But precious few of them exist today.   [635–6]

Blind hope and recklessness are both alike;
For both are harsh divinities to men.   [637–8]

Often the unplanned works of man succeed
Beyond all hope, while all their planning fails.   [639–40]

You'd never know your friends or enemies
If they weren't tried in serious affairs.   [641–2]

Beside the punch-bowl, many are loyal friends,
But in important matters, they are few.[30]   [643–4]

You'll find few helpful, faithful friends when you
Are really in the middle of distress.   [645–6]

The sense of shame has disappeared from men
And shamelessness roams over all the earth.   [647–8]

O wretched Poverty, why do you sit
Upon my shoulders, bringing me disgrace
In mind and body? I, who know the good
And beautiful, of all men, I have learned
Many vile things from you, against my will.   [649–52]

May I be happy, Kurnos, dear to the gods,
That is the only excellence I want.   [653–4]

Kurnos, we all feel sorry for your luck,
But another's grief lasts only for a day.   [655–6]

Don't be too grieved in bad times, nor too glad
In good; a gentleman bears everything.   [657–8]

Don't ever swear, 'That thing will never be!'
The gods might take offence, and they have power
Over the end. For good may come from bad
And bad from good. The pauper, suddenly,
May become rich, and he who has great wealth
May in one night lose everything he had.
The wise man errs, and fame comes to the fool;
And though he's worthless, honour is his fate.   [659-66]

† Simonides, if I had my past wealth
I wouldn't be so grim in company
With gentlemen. But wealth has passed me by
And I am mute, from poverty. And yet
I know, far more than most, that we're adrift,
With white sails lowered, in the murky night
Beyond the Melian Sea.[31] They will not bale
Although the sea is washing over both
Our sides. The danger's great, and they do this:
They have deposed their pilot, a good man,
Who kept us safe and knew his business well;
They've seized the money; discipline is lost,
Fair sharing is no more, and porters are
The pilots now, the bad above the good;
I fear the waves will swallow up our ship.
This darkly-worded riddle's for the good,
But a smart bad man might know what I mean.[32]   [667-82]

* Many rich men are stupid, while the men
Who want fine things are worn by poverty.
Thus, neither group can act, the one held back
By lack of gold, the other, lack of sense.   [683-6]

It's not permitted for a mortal man
To judge the deathless gods, or fight with them.   [687-8]

One should not violate the inviolable
Nor do what would be better left undone.   [689-90]

I wish you a happy trip across the sea:
May Poseidon take you, to delight your friends.　　　[691-2]

Excess has ruined many a foolish man:
When goods appear it's hard to be moderate.　　　[693-4]

My soul: I cannot give you all you need;
Patience – beauty is loved by others, too.　　　[695-6]

When things go well, I have a lot of friends,
But few stay loyal when my luck is bad.　　　[697-8]

* Most men think gold the only blessing,
That nothing else is worth possessing:
Not Rhadamanthus' moderation,
Not even such imagination
As Sisyphus displayed in hell.
(*There* was a brain, as you know well;
He broke the locks on Hades' gates
By cozening that Queen who waits
For every man who lives and dies;
She dims their minds, she dulls their eyes;
No other man has pierced that cloud
Which hovers round the captive crowd
Of vanished souls; no man who went
Through Death's grim doorway ever spent
Another hour in earthly light,
Yet Sisyphus got out all right,
The schemer left the boundless black,
And sun and life received him back.)
But he would fail in times like ours;
And Nestor's great forensic powers,
Which once made lying words seem true
And golden – they'd be laughed at, too.
Not even speed is prized, these days;
Outrace the Harpies? Still no praise.
Run fast as Boreas' sons, or faster –

You think the world will call you master?
Believe me, lad, these people hold
No lord but cash, no god but gold.[33]   [699-718]

† He who has countless gold and silver, fields
Of corn-land, mules and horses is no more
Rich than the man who has just what he needs,
Comforts of belly and chest and feet, delight
From a boy or woman. When the time is right
And youth brings fitting pleasures, that is wealth
For mortals. No one takes his great estate
Down to the house of Hades when he goes;
No one can pay a ransom and escape
Death, grim disease, or the sad approach of age.[34]   [719-28]

The wings of Care are variegated: some
Men weep for life and some for trivial needs.   [729-30]

* Dear father Zeus, I'm willing for the gods
(If they insist) to let a villain love
His outrage, but I wish that, after that,
The criminal, who acts intentionally
And disregards the gods, would pay, himself,
The penalty for crime – not that the sins
Of fathers should bring sorrow to their sons
In later days. The evil father's sons
Who practise justice, son of Kronos, they
Who fear your anger, loving from the first
The Right among their fellow-citizens,
Should not be punished for their father's crimes.
I wish the gods agreed. But as things are,
Bad men escape, and others bear the brunt.   [731-42]

And this, king of the gods: how is it just
That he who keeps himself from unjust acts
And never violates a law or oath,
This just man finds no justice from the gods?[35]

What other mortal, looking on this man,
Learns honour for the gods? How should he feel
Seeing the wicked, reckless man who has
No fear of god or man, glutted with gold
Won violently, while honourable men
Wear out their lives in wretched poverty?   [743-52]

Dear friend, if you have learned from me, pursue
Your fortune honestly, avoiding wrong,
And always keep my words in mind. At last
You'll come to praise the wise advice you've learned.   [753-6]

May Zeus in heaven keep his strong right hand
Forever on this town to make it safe,
Likewise, the other blessed deathless gods.
Apollo, guide my singing and my thoughts,
May holy songs be heard from lyre and flute.
Let's pour libation to the gods and drink,
Enjoying talk and fellowship, without
Any alarm about the Median war.
This is the better way, to pass the time
In pleasure, free from worries, happily,
With hearts united, keeping far away
Bad spirits, painful age and final death.   [757-68]

* It isn't fitting that the Muses' man
And messenger should jealously preserve
His wisdom. He must spend his time three ways:
Learning, teaching, composing – after all,
What good is knowledge if just one man knows?   [769-72]

† Lord Phoebus, you who built the towers of our
Acropolis, to please Alcathoos
The son of Pelops, now protect this town
From the outrageous army of the Medes
So that your people, when the Spring returns,
May give you glorious hecatombs,[36] with joy,

123

Delighting in the cithara[37] and feasts
With dancing in your honour, and with cries
Of gladness round your altar. I'm afraid,
Seeing the mindless lack of unity
Which weakens the Greek people. Phoebus, please
Favour this city, keep us in your care.   [773-82]

* One time I went to Sicily, and once
I visited Euboia's plains, where vines
Grow all around, and Sparta, glorious town
On the Eurotas River, lush with reeds,
And everywhere men loved and welcomed me:
But no delight came to my heart from them:
No country's dearer to me than my own.   [783-8]

I don't want any new pursuit, apart
From excellence and learning. I would like
Always to make these my concerns; then, too,
I want to find my pleasure in the lyre
And in the dance, and singing, and to keep
My mind alert, in noble company.   [789-92]

† Do not get into any mischief which
Might harm a foreigner or citizen,
Rejoice, in your own heart, at doing right;
Of your hard-hearted fellow-citizens
Some will revile you, others will speak well.[38]   [793-6]

The good are strongly blamed by some and praised
By others; no one thinks about the bad.   [797-8]

No one on earth can go uncriticized,
But don't be too much noticed; that is best.   [799-800]

No one has ever lived or yet will live
To please all men he meets before he dies.
Even the son of Kronos, Zeus, who rules
Men and immortals, can't please every one.[39]   [801-804]

Kurnos, the man who gets an oracle
From the priestess at the Pythian god's rich shrine[40]
Must scrutinize the answer carefully
As if he were a carpenter, with rule,
Compass, and square. For if you add one word
You're lost; and if you take away, you'll find
There's no escaping guilt in the gods' eyes.   [805-10]

I've suffered, Kurnos, something not quite worse
Than death, but painfuller than anything:
My friends betrayed me. Now I'm forced to be
With my enemies, I'll see how they behave.   [811-14]

An ox stamps hard with his foot upon my tongue,[41]
And I can't babble, even though I know.   [815-16]

Kurnos, there's no escape at all from fate;
What is my fate to suffer, I don't fear.   [817-18]

We've come to a bad time, Kurnos, time to pray
That Death might take us both at the same time.   [819-20]

My Kurnos, I have little time for those
Who don't respect their parents when they're old.   [821-2]

Don't help a tyrant for the sake of gain,
Don't kill one, if you've sworn your loyalty.   [823-4]

* How do you have the heart to sing to the flute?
You can see the border, from this market-place,
Of the land that feeds with her fruits the banqueters
All blond, with purple flowers in their hair.
Come, Scythian, cut your hair and stop the feast,
Mourn for the fragrant country you have lost.[42]   [825-30]

I lost my wealth through honour, got it back
Through lack of honour; two distasteful thoughts!   [831-2]

125

Everything's gone to the dogs and ruin![43] Still,
Kurnos, we must not blame the blessed gods:
The violence of men, vile greed and pride
Have thrown us from our good luck into bad.   [833-6]

Two demons of wine exist for us poor men:
Enfeebling Thirst and wretched Drunkenness.
I twist about, avoiding both; you won't
Persuade me to stay sober, or get drunk.   [837-40]

Wine pleases me at most times, but not when
It arms and leads me to my enemy.
But when it gets the upper hand, it's time
For me to stop my drinking and go home.   [841-4]

A man's good luck can easily be spoiled;
But to improve bad luck is difficult.   [845-6]

* Stamp on the empty-headed people! Jab
With your pointed goad, and lay the heavy yoke
Around their necks! You won't find, under the sun,
A people who love slavery so much.   [847-50]

Olympian Zeus; I pray, destroy that man
Who cheats his friend by murmuring soft words.   [851-2]

I knew it, but I know it better now:
There is no gratitude in common men.   [853-4]

Often, this city, like a ship off course,
Steered badly, has run much too close to land.   [855-6]

If any friend of mine sees me distressed
He turns his head away, and doesn't see,
But if I have a bit of rare good luck,
Dozens of hugs and kisses fall on me.   [857-60]

My friends betray me, give me nothing when
Men are around. So, of my own accord
I'll come out in the evening, and go back
At dawn, when all the roosters start to crow.[44]   [861-4]

The gods give wealth to many a worthless man
Which does no good to him nor to his friends;
But the great name of courage never dies:
The hero saves his city and its land.   [865-8]

May the great broad sky of bronze fall on my head
(That fear of earth-born men) if I am not
A friend to those who love me, and a pain
And irritation to my enemies.   [869-72]

Dear wine: I praise and blame you. I cannot
Entirely hate, nor love you totally.
You are both good and bad, and who could blame
Or praise you, if he had a bit of sense?   [873-6]

* Be young, my soul! New souls will soon abound,
And soon I'll be inanimate black ground.   [877-8]

Come, drink the wine which came to me from vines
Which aged Theotimus, the gods' friend,
Raised on the mountainside, beneath the peak
Of Taygetus, and brought cold water from
The springs of Platanistus for those vines.
And when you drink, you'll shed anxiety;
When you're well-armed, you'll feel as light as air.   [879-84]

May Peace and Wealth prevail, so I can feast
With friends. I'm not in love with evil war.   [885-6]

Don't pay attention to the herald's shouts:
It's not our native land for which we fight.   [887-8]

It would be shameful not to mount behind
The rapid horses, and face tearful war.   [889-90]

Oh, feebleness! Cerinthus is no more,
The vineyards of Lelantus are destroyed,
The good have fled, the bad control the town,
May Zeus destroy the race of Cypselids![45]   [891-4]

Nothing's more valuable for man than sense
And nothing, Kurnos, worse than foolishness.   [895-6]

If Zeus took mortal actions seriously,
Since he knows the inward thoughts of every man
And all the deeds of just and unjust men
It would be devastating for mankind.   [897-900]

Someone is better, someone worse in each
Pursuit; but no one's good at everything.   [901-902]

† The wise approve most highly any man
Who watches his expenditures, but still
Has fun.[46] If we could see our term of life,
And know how long we have before we cross
Over to Hades, we'd know what to do:
One who expected longer life could hold
His spending down, and have enough to last.
But we don't have this knowledge. As for me,
I'm wretched, torn apart, and of two minds –
I'm standing at the crossroads, wondering
Which of two paths to take: the first, to spend
Nothing, and live my life in misery
Or, to live pleasantly, accomplishing
Little. For I have seen a man who lived
So stingily, though he was rich, that he
Never would give his belly a free man's food –
He died untimely, went to Hades' house;
An insignificant heir got all his gold.
He suffered vainly, and he didn't give

To anyone he cared about. I've seen
Another man, who fed his belly well;
He used up all his money, then he said:
'It's been a lot of fun!' But now he begs
From all his friends, from everyone he meets.
So, Democles, it's best to have a care,
And live within our means. This is the way
Neither to give some other man the fruits
Of all your labours, nor to end your life
In the servitude of beggary. If you
Come to old age, your money won't run out.
These days, it's best to have some money. If
You're rich, you've lots of friends; if poor, you have
Few – and you're not a gentleman any more.   [903-30]

It's best to save: no one will mourn your death
Unless you've left a lot of cash behind.   [931-2]

Ability and looks fall to few men:
He has rare luck who gets them both combined.
Everyone honours him; the young, the old
And those of his own age give way to him.
When old, he's still a prominent citizen
Never deprived of justice or respect.[47]   [933-8]

* I can't sing sweetly, like the nightingale;
Because of last night's party. I don't blame
The flutist for my excuse – it's just my voice,
Usually fine, which has deserted me.   [939-42]

I'll stand beside the flutist, on his right
And sing an invocation to the gods.   [943-4]

I'll walk a straight true path and not incline
To either side; my thinking must be sure.
I'll put my native land in order, rule
This shining city, neither flattering
The mob, nor listening to the criminals.   [945-8]

• I'm like a lion, confident of power,
  Who, with his claws, has seized a fawn away
  From the mother doe, but doesn't drink its blood.
  I've climbed the ramparts, but not sacked the town;
  I've yoked the chariot's team, not mounted it;
  Acting, I haven't acted; finishing,
  I've finished nothing. Nothing is complete
  Though I've completed much; accomplishing,
  I've not accomplished anything at all.[48]   [949–54]

Lend to a low-born man and you will get
Two blows: the loss of money and no thanks.   [955–6]

If you don't thank me for this favour, just
Try knocking at my door another time!   [957–8]

• When I drank alone at that black-watered spring,
  The water tasted clean and sweet to me;
  But now it is polluted, mixed with mud,
  I'll go to other sources for my drinks.   [959–62]

Don't praise a man till you can clearly see
The rhythm of his ways, his character.
Many a cheat will put on a disguise,
And have a pleasing manner for the day,
But time will show the nature of the man.
I was unwise in this: for I praised you
Too soon, before I knew your character –
Now, like a ship, I'm going to sail away . . .[49]   [963–70]

To win a drinking contest – what's it worth?
The bad man often beats the good in that.   [971–2]

Nobody, when the earth once covers him
And he goes down to Erebos, the house
Of Queen Persephone, can take delight
In hearing flute or lyre, or in the gifts

Of Dionysus. Knowing this, I plan
To satisfy my heart, while I have limbs
Still nimble, and no shaking of the head.   [973-8]

A man who's friend in word but not in deed
Is not my friend: he must give help to me
With hands and money both, not warm my heart
With words beside the mixing-bowl; he must
Prove, if he can, by action, that he's good.   [979-82]

* Let's give our hearts to banqueting, while we
Can still find pleasure in delightful things.
For glorious youth goes by as fast as thought,
Faster than horses charging recklessly
Bringing their master to the work of war,
While they delight in the smooth wheat-bearing plain.   [983-8]

Drink when the others drink. When you're depressed
Let no one see your heaviness of heart.   [989-990]

* Sometimes you'll be delighted when you act,
Sometimes, distressed when others act on you:
No one can be the actor all the time.   [991-2]

Academus, if you challenge me to sing
A lovely song, and set out as the prize
For this artistic contest, a young man
In the full bloom of beauty, you will learn
How much more strong a mule is than an ass.50   [993-6]

When the Sun has led his smooth-hooved horses past
The middle sky at noontime, let's enjoy
Our dinner as we wish to, and let's give
Our bellies every sort of luscious food,
With holy water quickly taken out
And garlands carried in by the soft hands
Of a beautiful Laconian serving-girl.   [997-1002]

131

† For a wise man this is excellence, the prize
  Most honoured, and the noblest one to win,
  And good for both the people and the state:
  To stand in the front ranks, immovable.⁵¹   [1003–1006]

  I will advise all men: while you still have
  The glorious flower of youth and noble thoughts,
  Enjoy these precious goods. To be young twice
  Is not permitted mortals by the gods,
  Nor to be free from death; vile Age will come,
  Destructive, and will put us to the test,
  And lay his hands on top of all our heads.   [1007–12]

* O happy, lucky, rich, the man who dies
  And goes to Hades' gloomy house without
  Experiencing trials such as these:
  Cringing before an enemy; being forced
  To do a wrong; testing the faith of friends.   [1013–16]

† A strange and sudden sweat runs down my skin;
  I tremble, seeing young men of my age
  In the flower of youth as sweet as it is fair;
  I wish it could last longer; but it goes
  Fast as a dream, this honoured Youth, and Age,
  The Shapeless Killer, hangs close over us.⁵²   [1017–22]

  Not if they put Mount Tmolus on my head
  Would I bow my neck to my enemies' heavy yoke.   [1023–4]

  In bad times, common men get sillier;
  But gentlemen can stand up straighter still.   [1025–6]

  Kurnos, for men it's easy to do wrong;
  But planning a good deed is difficult.   [1027–8]

* Be brave, my soul, although in these hard times
  You suffer things unbearable. The hearts
  Of common men are quick to be distressed.

Don't make your pain the worse by worrying
About what can't be done; don't vex yourself,
Don't grieve your friends and please your enemies.
A mortal man can't easily escape
The destined gifts of gods, not if he goes
To the very bottom of the purple sea
Nor if he lies in misty Tartarus.   [1029–36]

It's very hard to fool an honest man;
A long time, Kurnos, I've been clear on this.   [1037–8]

I knew it, but I know it better now:
There is no gratitude in common men.[53]   [1038a–b]

Those men are silly fools who do not drink
When the Dog Star is upon us, lots of wine!   [1039–40]

You and the flutist, come! We'll laugh and drink
Near the weeper, and enjoy his agonies.   [1041–2]

† Let's sleep: the guardians of our peaceful town
Our well-loved land, will keep sufficient watch.   [1043–4]

If one of them's asleep and covered up,
By Zeus! he will enjoy our serenade!   [1045–6]

For now let's drink, enjoy ourselves, and speak
Fine words: the gods will see to what comes next.   [1047–8]

As father to son, I give this excellent
Advice to you; so bear it well in mind:
Never be hasty or you'll make mistakes.
Think carefully – consult your deepest thoughts
And your good brain. The minds and hearts of fools
Flit here and there but thinking benefits
Even the very keen intelligence.   [1049–54]

Let's stop this talking, and you play the flute;
Let's both remember the Muses, for they bring
The loveliest gifts for you and me to have
Also, for neighbours hearing us, to share. [1055-8]

Timagoras, even a wise man finds
It's hard to know most men, seen from far-off;
Some keep their badness hid by wealth, and some
Their goodness hid by wretched poverty. [1059-62]

† When he's young, a man can sleep the whole night long
With a friend of his own age, and have his fill
Of making love, and he can join the flute
And sing, and go to parties. Nothing else
Is so delightful to a boy or girl.
What do I care for honour or for wealth?
Pleasure and happiness beat everything. [1063-8]

Those men are silly fools who mourn the dead
And do not mourn the flower of lost youth. [1069-70]

Be happy, soul: new souls will soon abound
And soon I'll be inanimate black ground.[54] [1070a-b]

My soul: be changeable with all your friends,
Adapt yourself to each one's mood and style;
Now, be like this, and then, behave like that:
Cleverness conquers even excellence.[55] [1071-4]

It's very hard to know how God will end
Events yet unperformed. We cannot see
Where our perplexity will stop, before
The future happens. Darkness covers us. [1075-8]

I'll blame no enemy who's honourable,
Nor praise a friend who acts in a low way. [1079-80]

134

This city's pregnant, Kurnos, and I fear
She'll bear a violent leader of civil war;
The people still have sense, but those in charge
Are turning, stumbling into evil ways.[56]　　　　[1081-82b]

Oh Kurnos, if you love me as you say
Don't cuddle up with words and let your mind
Go wandering elsewhere; either keep your thoughts
Wholly for me, or tell me now, straight out,
You hate me; quarrel, and let our break be clean.[57]　　[1082c-f]

A gentleman must always keep his thoughts
Directed steadfastly towards his friend.　　　　[1083-4]

It's hard, Demonax, for you to bear too much;
You've never learned to do what you don't like.　　[1085-6]

Castor and Pollux, you who live in divine
Lacedaemon, by the lovely flowing stream
Eurotas, if I ever give a friend
Bad counsel, let me suffer his results.
If he does it to me, let him pay twice.　　　　[1087-90]

* My heart's uneasy with your love. I can't
Hate you or love you. Since we have been friends
It's difficult to hate you. All the same,
It's hard to love you when you don't love me.　　[1091-4]

Find someone else; I'm not obliged to help –
Where are your thanks for what I did before?　　[1095-6]

I'll fly like a bird away from the stagnant marsh
Escaping an evil man by breaking the net.
But as for you, who spoiled our friendship; you
Will understand, too late, how wise I was.　　[1097-1100]

... Whoever has advised you about me,
And told you to betray our love and go ...[58]　　[1101-1102]

Pride has destroyed Magnesia, Colophon,
And Smyrna. Certainly, she will destroy
You too, my Kurnos, and those friends of yours.   [1103-1104]

Reputation's an evil; trial is best.
Many have good repute that are untried.[59]
Put to the test, like gold beside mere lead[60]
You will be seen by all, refined and pure.   [1104a-1106]

What a wretch I am! A joy to my enemies,
A burden to my friends, through suffering.   [1107-8]

The gentlemen of old are now the trash;
The trash are nobles, Kurnos; who can bear
To see the good dishonoured and the bad
Honoured? Now gentlemen court common girls;
These people cheat each other and they laugh,
They haven't any principles at all.[61]   [1109-14]

I toss about in problems, anxiously:
I've yet to escape the kingdom of Poverty.[62]   [1114a-b]

You, rich man, criticize my poverty:
But I still have some property, and will,
Relying on the gods, obtain still more.   [1115-16]

Hail, Ploutos, finest of gods and most beloved!
With you, a serf becomes a gentleman.[63]   [1117-18]

May I have my share of youth; may I be loved
By Phoebus Apollo, Leto's son, and Zeus
King of the gods, so I may live with Right
Far from all evils, happy in youth and wealth.   [1119-22]

Oh, don't remind me of my troubles. I
Have suffered like Odysseus. He escaped
From the great house of Hades and came back

To kill, without remorse and eagerly,
The suitors of his wife Penelope
Who waited long for him, with her dear son
Till he returned . . .[64]   [1123-8]

I'll drink, and forget soul-wasting Poverty,
And all the enemies who slander me.
I do mourn lovely Youth, which goes from me
And weep that painful Age is coming fast.   [1129-32]

Kurnos, let's stop this evil among our friends
Before it starts; let's try to find a drug
To heal the sore before it comes to a head.   [1133-4]

Hope is the one good god still left on earth;
The rest forsake us and have gone to live
On Mount Olympus. Gone is the great god Trust
And Wisdom's gone; my friend, the Graces have
Abandoned earth. Firm oaths no longer stand,
And no one worships the immortal gods.
The race of pious men has died away
And no one now knows reverence or law.
Yet, while a man's alive and sees the sun,
Let him still worship Hope among the gods
And let him pray, and burn rich offerings
To the gods, and let him sacrifice to Hope
The first and last. Let him be on his guard
Against the crooked words of criminals
Who don't revere the gods, but set their hearts
Always upon the goods of other men,
Conspiring shamefully for evil ends.   [1135-50]

Never listen to common men and seek
Another friend, forsaking one you have.[65]   [1151-2]

May I be rich and live an innocent life
Free from all evil, far from anxieties.   [1153-4]

† I don't desire or pray for wealth; may I
Live, free from evil, on a small amount.   [1155-6]

Wisdom and wealth are the hardest things for man
To conquer. Wealth, because you never have
Enough. The same is true of wisdom, for
The wisest man can't turn away from it,
But loves it passionately, and can't be filled.   [1157-60]

You young men, now! I'm not obliged to help –
Where are your thanks for what I did before?[66]   [1160a-b]

Kurnos, don't lay up treasures for your sons
But lend to gentlemen who are in need.   [1161-2]

No one is always lucky in all things;
Good men endure bad luck without complaint,
The common man cannot control himself
In good times or in bad. All sorts of gifts
Come to us mortals from the gods; we must
Endure, whatever sorts of gifts they give.[67]   [1162a-f]

The eyes and tongue and ears and mind of a man
Stay locked inside his chest if he is wise.   [1163-4]

Find yourself friends who understand your moods
And brother-like, bear with your grouchiness.
If you will give your mind to what I say
Dear friend, you will remember me, one day.[68]   [1164a-d]

Searching, I've found no comrade like myself,
A faithful friend, in whom there's no deceit.
Put to the test, like gold beside mere lead,
I will be found superior every time.[69]   [1164e-h]

Mingle with gentlemen, avoid the low,
When, on a business trip, you're far from home.   [1165-6]

A good man answers well and his acts are good;
The bad man's worthless words fly on the wind.   [1167-8]

Bad comes from bad companionship; you'll learn
This well, for you've offended the great gods.   [1169-70]

The gods give nothing better to a man
Than sense, Kurnos; with sense, a man controls
The outcome of all action. He who has
Sense in his thoughts is lucky, for it is
Stronger than evil pride and wretched greed.
There's no worse thing for mortal men than greed;
Greed, Kurnos, is the source of every wrong.   [1171-6]

If you never did or suffered shameful things,
Kurnos, you'd make a start at being good.   [1177-8]

The man whose heart's in trouble must be brave
And ask the deathless gods for his release.[70]   [1178a-b]

Kurnos, respect and fear the gods; you'll be
Prevented from bad deeds and impious speech.   [1179-80]

If you should overthrow, by any means
A tyrant who devours the people, know
No vengeance from the gods will fall on you.   [1181-2]

The Sun whose rays illuminate mankind
Sees no one, Kurnos, who's untouched by blame.   [1183-4]

I cannot understand these citizens,
Can't please them, whether I do good or harm.[71]   [1184a-b]

The mind and tongue are precious: just a few
Know how to be good managers of both.   [1185-6]

No one by paying ransom can escape
Death or misfortune, if it's not his fate.
Nor can a man escape anxiety
By bribery, when God sends pain to him.   [1187-90]

* Don't lay me out, when I'm dead, on a royal couch,
I'd like some good things while I'm still alive.
Boughs are as good as carpets for a corpse
To lie on: wood's not hard or soft to him.   [1191-4]

Do not swear falsely by the gods. You can't
Cover up any debt you owe to them.   [1195-6]

* I heard the fall bird's shrill alarm, I heard
That call which bids the farmer plough his lands;
My heart was shattered by that crying bird:
My blooming pastures lie in other hands,
A stranger's mules are yoked to pull my plough –
Our state is led by hateful pilots now.[72]   [1197-1202]

* I will not go. No tyrant will be mourned
By me, nor will I wail for him at the tomb
When he goes underground, no more than he
Would feel distress for me if I were dead,
Or let fall from his eyelids the hot tears.   [1203-6]

* I won't invite you to the party, nor
Forbid you. When you're present, I'm distressed,
But when you go away, you still are loved.   [1207-8]

I come from Aethon's race, but now I live
In well-walled Thebes, exiled from my own land.[73]   [1209-10]

Don't make rude jokes and taunt me, Argyris,
With who my parents were: you were a slave.
I've had my troubles, woman, since I've been
Exiled, but never, dreadful slavery.

They don't sell men like me. And I still have
A city of my own – it's beautiful,
And situated near to Lethe's plain.74   [1211–16]

Let's never laugh, enjoying our good luck,
When, Kurnos, we sit next to one who grieves.   [1217–18]

Kurnos, it's hard to fool an enemy
But easy for a friend to cheat his friend.   [1219–20]

Words can lead men to error, frequently,
Kurnos, by putting confusion in their minds.75   [1221–22]

Nothing's worse, Kurnos, than bad temper, which
Harms by indulging a man's worse tendencies.   [1223–24]

† Nothing is pleasanter than a good wife;
I've proved it, Kurnos; now, you prove it, too.   [1225–26]

I'm called home by a cadaver from the sea.
Although it's dead, it speaks with living lips.76   [1227–30]

† Cruel Love, the demons of Madness took you up
And nursed you: you destroyed the tallest towers
Of Ilium, destroyed great Theseus,
Aegeus' son, and through your recklessness
Good Ajax, son of Oileus, was lost.   [1231–4]

Boy, get hold of yourself; listen to me:
I'll speak convincing words, and pleasing ones.
So try to understand: there is no need
For you to do a thing that you don't wish.   [1235–8]

Never listen to common men and seek
Another friend, forsaking one you have.77
To me, they've often slandered you; don't pay
Any attention when they slander me.   [1238a–40]

141

You'll long for your old love, when you can't be
The manager of the love that you have now.
Let's still be friends, but you, find other men [78]
And keep your slippery ways that damage trust.   [1241-4]

Fire doesn't mix with water. Nor will we
Ever be one another's faithful friends.   [1245-6]

Think of my hate and violence; rest assured
I will do all I can to punish you.   [1247-8]

* You're like a horse, boy, who has had his fill
Of barley elsewhere, then comes back to me,
Wanting a gentle rider, a cool spring,
Soft meadows to run in, and some shady woods.   [1249-52]

† He's lucky who has boyfriends, and smooth-hooved
Horses and hunting dogs and foreign friends. [79]   [1253-4]

That man is never happy who does not
Love dogs and smooth-hooved horses and young men.   [1255-6]

My boy, you're just like a wandering water-bird
Flying now here, now there, in search of love. [80]   [1257-8]

You're lovely to look at, boy, but on your head
There lies a heavy crown of silliness.
You're like a kite, you wheel around so fast
Persuaded by the words of other men.   [1259-62]

Boy, I've treated you well, and you give back
Evil in turn; I get no thanks from you.
You've never helped me; I who have helped you
So often, don't have even your respect.   [1263-6]

* Horses and boys are the same. The horse does not
Weep for his rider lying in the dust,
But carries another man and eats his grain;
A boy, too, only loves his current friend.   [1267-70]

Boy, you've driven me crazy with your greed;
You're an embarrassment to all our friends.
But after this storm, you're giving me a rest;
Night's coming; I'll drop anchor quietly.   [1271-4]

† Love comes in season, when the pregnant earth
Bursts forth with blooming flowers of the Spring;
Then leaving Cyprus, beautiful island, love
Comes to the men on earth, and brings them joy.   [1275-8]

... Whoever has advised you about me
And told you to betray our love and go ...[81]   [1278a-b]

I'm like a lion, confident of power,
Who, with his claws, has seized a fawn away
From the mother doe, but doesn't drink its blood.[82]   [1278c-d]

* I wouldn't do you harm, my handsome boy,
Not even if the gods rewarded it.
I do not sit as a judge of petty crimes;
No handsome boys exist who haven't strayed.   [1279-82]

† Don't wrong me; I still want to please you, boy,
But hear and understand this with good grace:
You won't deceive or fool me with your tricks;
For now you've won, and have the upper hand,
But I will wound you as you run away
From me, if you should run as once, they say
Iasius' virgin daughter ran, to flee
Marriage which she despised, though ripe for it.
Blonde Atalanta armed herself and did
The impossible; she left her father's house
And climbed the highest mountains, to escape
Delightful marriage, Aphrodite's gift.
But though she fought, she married, in the end.   [1283-94]

143

Don't toss my heart, boy, into cruel pains,
Don't let our love conduct me to the house
Of Queen Persephone. Be kind, respect
The anger of the gods and the talk of men.   [1295–8]

How long, boy, will you run away, and I
Pursue? I hope I'll see some end to this
Anger of yours. But you with your haughty heart
And greed, keep flying, like a cruel kite.
Stay, and oblige me, for the violet-crowned
Cyprian's gift will not be yours too long.   [1299–304]

You know in your heart the blooming of lovely youth
Goes quicker than a race: think about this
And free me from these chains, thou mighty boy,[83]
In fear that some day you'll be chained yourself
And face the punishments of the Cyprian
As now I do. Be on your guard, my boy,
Or misery like mine will conquer you.   [1305–10]

You haven't fooled me, boy, with your deceit.
I see right through you; you're so very close
And loving now, with some, for whom you've thrown
My love aside as worthless – but these men
Are ones you never even liked before.
I once thought you, of all my friends, could be
Faithful, but now you love another man.
I, who did well by you, am tossed aside:
I hope men see, and quit the love of boys!   [1311–18]

What a wretch I am! A joy to my enemies,
A burden to my friends, through suffering.[84]   [1318a–b]

Since Cypris made you charming, boy, and all
The young men are obsessed with your good looks,
Hear my advice, and thank me with your heart,
Knowing how heavy a burden is man's love.   [1319–22]

Cyprian, stop my pains; scatter abroad
My heart-devouring worries; turn me back
To joy, and put an end to evil grief.
Then when I've had my share of happy youth,
Let me go on to wise and sober work.   [1323-6]

As long as your cheek's so smooth, my boy, I won't
Stop kissing you, you wouldn't even stop
If the punishment for doing so were death.   [1327-8]

* It's beautiful for you to give to me,
And since I love you, no disgrace for me
To beg. I pray you, by your knees and hands
Honour me, handsome boy, do what I ask;
For some day you will face another boy
And want the violet-crowned Cyprian's gift;
May you receive the same response I've had!   [1329-34]

Happy the lover who exercises, then
Goes home to sleep all day with a handsome boy.   [1335-6]

* I'm finished with that boy! I've kicked out dull
Grief, and escaped hard labour, happily.
Crowned Cytherea freed me from desire
And now, my boy, you have no charm for me.   [1337-40]

I love a smooth-skinned boy, who shows me off
Against my will, to all his friends. Oh well,
I'll let them stare at these indignities;
They'll see I serve a not unworthy boy.   [1341-4]

† The love of boys is sweet. Even the king
Of gods, the son of Kronos, loved a boy
Ganymede, and he took him to his home
Olympus, and he gave divinity
To him, because he had the lovely bloom
Of youth. Don't be surprised, Simonides,
To see me love and serve a handsome boy.[85]   [1345-50]

Don't go to the drinking-party, boy; believe
This old man's wisdom: drinking's not for the young. [1351-2]

Bitter and sweet and smooth and rough is love
For the young man, Kurnos, till it's satisfied.
When satisfied, it's sweet. If you pursue
But don't get what you want, it's miserable. [1353-6]

Upon the necks of the lovers of boys, there is
Always a heavy yoke, a painful thing
To remind them of their open-heartedness. [1357-8]

If you'd lead a boy to love, you will be burned
As if you'd put your hand in a fire of twigs. [1359-60]

In sinning against my love, you're like a ship
With hawsers rotten through, that strikes a rock. [1361-2]

I'll never hurt you, even when you're gone;
And no one can dissuade me from my love. [1363-4]

Most lovable and handsomest of boys;
Stay here and listen to some songs of mine. [1365-6]

There's gratitude in boys. A woman loves
Her current man; no loyalty's in her. [1367-8]

* The love of boys is fine to have, and fine
To leave - it is much easier to find
Than satisfy. Ten thousand evils come
From it; also ten thousand benefits;
But even this gives it a certain charm. [1369-72]

You never wait around for me, but if
A message comes, you're eager to be off. [1373-4]

The happy man's in love, and doesn't know
The sea, or fear night falling on the waves. [1375-6]

146

You're handsome, boy, but those bad friends of yours
Have led you to consort with vulgar men;
And now you're blamed for acting shamefully.
I who against my will have lost your love,
Have really profited: I'm free again.   [1377–80]

They thought you went to the altar with a gift
For the violet-crowned, golden Cyprian . . .[86]   [1381–2]

The hardest burden for a man to bear
Comes when the Cyprian fails to ease his pain.   [1383–5]

Sly Cytherea, born on Cyprus: Zeus
Gave you outstanding honour with this gift:
You overwhelm men's clever minds; no man
Is wise or strong enough to run from you.   [1386–8]

NOTES

Hesiod, *Theogony*

1. Literally, 'Why all this about oak or stone?' This must be a proverbial expression (perhaps in reference to a children's game, 'Here we go round the oak (or stone)!'), something like 'beating about the bush'. At any rate, it seems to refer to wasting time.

2. 'in harmony': the Greek is *homereusai*, which could, but does not, mean 'with Homeric voices'. Is it possible that here we find a clue to the meaning of Homer's name? The Homeridai (sons of Homer) were a guild of professional singers. Maybe their name originally meant 'harmonious men', 'sons of harmony', and the name Homer was invented for their eponymous founder, *then* applied to the author of the epics they sang. The major problem with this interpretation, of course, is that the Homeridai sang solo, but perhaps they originally sang in chorus, before they took to chanting Homer's popular works.

3. This section is just as stilted and repetitive in Greek as it is in English.

4. 'lords': the word *basileus* means 'king' in later Greek. But in Hesiod (particularly in the *Works and Days*), it seems to refer to any sort of leader or magistrate, or feudal 'lord'.

5. Space: *aither*, the pure upper atmosphere, as opposed to *aer*, which we mortals breathe.

6. *Cyclops* means 'round-eyed' (from *kuklos*, a circle) not 'one-eyed'.

7. Adamant is a mythical metal, harder than anything. Later identified with steel, or with diamonds.

8. Meliae: ash-tree nymphs. Dryads were oak-tree nymphs.

9. The name Aphrodite is here, probably incorrectly, connected with *aphros*, 'foam'.

10. Philommedes: 'genital-loving'. This might be a corruption of *philomeides*, 'laughter-loving', a more usual (and daintier) epithet of the goddess.
11. Titans: 'strainers' (from *teino*, I strain), another probably false etymology.
12. Ker: a spirit of death, often plural.
13. Although the relationship between Strife and Work is reminiscent of the *Works and Days*, the tone here is diametrically opposed.
14. Nereus is here connected with *nemertes* ('never wrong'), which seems a far-fetched etymology even for Hesiod.
15. In reading these Greek names it must be remembered that every syllable, including final 'e' is sounded: 'Amphitrite' is therefore four syllables.
16. Most of the Nereids' names have something to do with the sea or with their infallible father, and are quite transparently invented for the occasion. They fit nicely into dactylic hexameter, but not blank verse.
17. Poseidon.
18. *pegai*: 'springs, waters'.
19. *chrys*: 'gold'; *aor*: 'sword'.
20. It is not clear whether 'she' is Ceto, or Medusa, or Callirhoe. Probably Ceto.
21. The Arimoi might be a tribe, or a mountain range. See West, pp. 250–51.
22. Heracles, who is called 'the son of Amphitryon' (the mortal husband of his mother Alcmene), although he was really the son of Zeus.
23. Another ambiguous 'she'. It is impossible to tell whether Hydra or Echidna is the mother here; the ancients were as confused as we are.
24. The Sun, the Moon and the Dawn.
25. 'Early-born': an epithet of the Dawn, Eos.
26. This is a graceful image, one of the few really poetic lines in the work.
27. Another good line, and so soon after the last one, too.
28. Hekate here is not the witch-goddess (associated with magic,

death, and the moon) of later literature, but a particularly powerful and benign personal deity. Perhaps, as West suggests, Hesiod's father, who came from Asia Minor, learned Hekate-worship in Miletus, an early centre of her cult. If he did, says West, 'It will be no coincidence that he gave one of his sons the name Perses, the name which Hesiod attributes to Hekate's father.' (*Hesiod, Theogony*, M. L. West, ed., p. 278.)

29. Poseidon.

30. Hephaistos.

31. A battle-cry.

32. The word *horkos*, usually translated 'oath', has a meaning for which English has no word. It is, here, the thing sworn by or on. We do swear by things, of course ('on a stack of bibles'; 'by my mother's head') but we have no word for the magical or revered object.

33. Athene.

34. This is perhaps the point at which the genuine work of Hesiod ends.

35. Usually, the Horae (Hours) are the seasons. West (p. 406) thinks they are deities who protect agriculture, and that Hesiod may here have invented their individual names, to show that agricultural productivity depends on political stability.

36. The work breaks off at this point. But the last part of the work (perhaps from line 900, note 34) is not generally thought to be by Hesiod, and seems to have been added to provide a transition to the *Catalogue of Women*.

Hesiod, *Works and Days*

1. Literally 'mallow and asphodel', both cheap vegetables. In the *Odyssey* (Book 11), the shades of dead heroes are encountered in a meadow of asphodel, and this association with the after-life reappears in later poets and becomes more usual than Hesiod's practical usage.
2. Prometheus.
3. Pandora means 'all the gifts' or 'gifts from all'.
4. Epimetheus means 'Hindsight'; his brother was Prometheus ('Foresight').
5. Hesiod leaves it ambiguous as to whether Hope is the one solace left for men in the now troubled world, or simply one more of the troubles brought by woman. The Greeks did not generally speak well of hope: her constant epithet is *tuphlos* – 'blind'.
6. This phrase is somewhat uncertain; perhaps it means 'with spears made of ash'.
7. Shame should perhaps be called 'the sense of shame' or 'honour'. Hesiod and Homer lived in what the anthropologists call a shame culture (as opposed to a guilt culture, like ours). The chief reason for good behaviour in a shame culture is the fear of what other people will think, i.e. the sense of shame. Thus Shame is a good goddess. For more on this topic, see Ruth Benedict, *The Chrysanthemum and the Sword*, and E. R. Dodds, *The Greeks and the Irrational*.
8. In early May. This is the early morning (heliacal) rising. See Sinclair, p. 42.
9. In November.
10. In October.

11. I believe that height, not width is indicated. A round tree is being cut up; the farmer is instructed about the lengths to cut, not the diameter. But see Sinclair, pp. 45–6.

12. It is unclear just what these words mean, but I have received the following plausible suggestion from a reader, Mr Rob Backhouse: 'If the "eight-slice loaf" is an eight-portion loaf, a loaf which feeds eight, then to dine on such a loaf quartered means "to eat as much as two". In the context (or perhaps simply as a saying of the times) means "who'll do the work of two".'

13. In October.

14. In December.

15. In March.

16. The name of a month. It covered late January and early February.

17. The octopus.

18. The Ethiopians or Egyptians in Africa.

19. February to March.

20. The snail: in mid-May.

21. July.

22. A burglar.

23. September.

24. October.

25. Late August.

26. All this word-play is present in the original: perhaps one of the rare moments of something like humour in Hesiod.

27. Hesiod is not thinking of etiquette but of a possible offence to the god Helios, the sun, and then, to other gods of the road and the night. Similarly, in the following verses, it is Hestia, the virgin goddess of the hearth-fire, who would be annoyed at the man's exhibitionism.

28. These astonishing verses refer to cutting the finger-nails in public.

29. Again Hesiod is not concerned with etiquette or sanitary precautions; he is afraid the river god or the god of the sea will be insulted.

30. The month is divided into two parts, the waxing and the waning moon, not into three parts as in later times. Thus assuming a month of thirty days, the 'midmonth fourth' would be the nineteenth of the month. But sometimes Hesiod uses the dates as we do.

31. The ant.

32. Perhaps this should be twenty-ninth. The Greek says 'three nines', which has been interpreted as the third ninth, in a three-part month. But Hesiod does not use a three-part month; therefore, either this means three times nine, or the lines are a later addition to the poem.

Theognis, *Elegies*

1. The first two poems are addressed to the god Apollo, the third to his sister Artemis, the fourth to the Muses and Graces. None of these is generally considered to be by Theognis.
2. Scholars disagree about this 'seal'. Literally, Theognis says 'Kurnos, let a seal (as in a signet ring) be on these words.' Some think the seal is the poet's name, some the excellence of his writing. I have indicated my opinion (the commonest one) by my translation: the seal is the name of Kurnos, which marks the genuine work of Theognis. In fact, it has worked pretty well; there are perhaps some Kurnos poems in this collection which are not by Theognis, and there are certainly many non-Kurnos poems which *are* by Theognis, but the name of his protégé is still a fairly good test of authenticity.
3. The 'sense of shame', *aidos*, is as important a virtue for Theognis as it is for Hesiod. For the early Greeks, shame – the fear that one's peers would think badly of one – was what kept men from wrongdoing. It is still the dominant value in most non-European cultures. cf. Hesiod, *Works and Days*, 198–202 and note 7.
4. This is by Solon, very slightly altered.
5. *daimon*: a sort of patron spirit, somewhat like the Roman 'genius' of a man.
6. I have translated this rather freely. Here is a more literal prose version:

    In rams and asses and horses, Kurnos, we select the well-born; one wishes to acquire offspring of good stock. But in marriage a gentleman doesn't care whether his wife is lowborn, and from a lowborn father, if the father gives him plenty of money. Nor does a woman refuse to be the wife of a lowborn man if he's rich; she wants money rather than excellence. They all want money; thus, gentlemen breed with low families, low ones with noble. Wealth has mongrelized (mixed up) breeding (the race). Thus, don't be surprised, son of Polypaos, if our citizens' children come to nothing, for good is mingled with bad.

7. A more literal prose version:

Behave like the intricate polyp (cuttlefish), which appears to the eye the same as the rock he's fixed to. At one time behave this way; at another, change complexion in that direction. Cleverness is stronger than consistency.

8. This is a slightly changed version of a poem by Solon.
9. The text here is difficult.
10. Prose version:

I have given you wings, with which you will fly, lifted easily over the boundless sea and the whole earth. At every feast and banquet you'll be present, lying on the lips of many, and the lovely young men will sing, gracefully, clear and beautiful songs about you to the clear-voiced flutes. And when you go down under the depths of the dark earth, to the house of Hades filled with weeping, even though you are dead, your fame will not die; you will be dear to men, having an undying name forever, Kurnos; travelling over the Greek land and the islands, crossing the fishy, barren sea, not carried on horseback, but the glorious gifts of the violet-crowned Muses will send you to all men who care for you, and you will be a song to men of the future, so long as Earth and Sun exist. But as for me, I don't get any respect from you; you cheat me with stories as if I were a little child.

11. An enigma, or riddle poem, of which Theognis wrote several. One possible solution is that the horse and rider are a city and her tyrant.
12. The solution to this enchanting riddle is offered by Carrière. It is a waterjug (jealous of a handsomer winejar), carried by a girl who moans when the cold wet 'lip' of the jug 'kisses' her as she staggers with it.
13. Text uncertain.
14. By Solon.
15. = ll. 209-10.

16. In prose:

O Olympian Zeus, accomplish my just prayer: give me some good
instead of bad. May I die if I don't find some release from these evil
worries, and may I pay back sorrow for sorrow. This would be fair;
but no vengeance appears for me on those men who have my prop-
erty, wrested away by force. I, a dog, crossed the torrent, but lost
everything in the stormy river. May I drink their black blood! May
some good daimon arise to accomplish this to my liking.

17. More textual problems.
18. I have omitted the next three lines. I agree with Carrière and
others that they are an interpolation, added by someone other
than Theognis to clarify the preceding, probably incomplete
poem. In prose, they read: 'But the good man should endure
and bear these things; he should respect his friends and avoid
man-destroying oaths, cleverly defending himself against the
gods' anger.'
19. See note 5.
20. See note 3.
21. The children of Asclepius are doctors.
22. This was apparently written by Euenos.
23. = ll. 211–12.
24. Ploutos – the god of money.
25. The 'voiceless messenger' is a beacon light.
26. This couplet and the next, obviously related, are rather
mysterious.
27. This is by Solon, somewhat changed.
28. *Poikilon*, which I have translated 'slippery', means both
'speckled' and 'devious'.
29. cf. ll. 133–42.
30. See ll. 115–16.
31. Beyond the Melian Sea would be dangerous, open waters.
32. This is probably by Euenos.
33. In prose:

To most men this is the one excellence: to be rich. Nothing else is
worth anything, not if you had the good judgement of Rhadaman-
thus, nor if you were more intelligent than Sisyphus the son of
Aeolus, who with his cleverness escaped from Hades, having

persuaded Persephone with flattering words – Persephone who gives men oblivion by damaging their minds. (No one else had ever plotted to do this, when once the black cloud of death covered him and he went to the shadowy place of the dead, and passed the dark gates which imprison the souls of the dead against their will. But Sisyphus the hero came back even from there to the light of the sun, through his own cunning.) Not if you could make lies seem true, having the tongue of godlike Nestor, not if you were faster on foot than the swift Harpies, or the sons of Boreas, whose feet are so quick. No; it is necessary for all to learn this wisdom: wealth has the greatest power among all men.

34. Solon again.
35. The multiple variations on the word 'just' are present in the Greek, too.
36. Hecatomb – a large sacrifice.
37. Cithara – a stringed instrument, ancestor of the zither.
38. Mimnermus wrote this.
39. cf. ll. 25–6.
40. The oracle of Apollo, at Delphi.
41. Proverbial for forced silence.
42. Scythian – a primitive person, without patriotic feelings. Theognis berates his fellow exiles for enjoying themselves, when they are so close to their homeland they can see its border, and can imagine the lower-class (blond) inhabitants feasting and carousing, eating the confiscated fruits of the land.
43. 'To the dogs'. The Greek is 'to the crows'. It means the same thing.
44. Another riddle poem. The speaker is feminine, perhaps a prostitute's cat, perhaps the Moon (to whom sacrifice was given at night).
45. Cypselids: the sons of Cypselus. The references here are puzzling. Cypselus overthrew the democracy of Corinth in about 655 and reigned till 625; the reigns of his son Periander and his grandnephew Cypselus II lasted till about 580 – in other words, they were probably finished before Theognis' day. They had no known connection with Euboia, where Cerinthus and the Lelantine vineyards are. Perhaps, as Car-

rière suggests (pp. 124–5), the Cypselids here are the family of the Athenian Miltiades.

46. Reading χρήματ' ἀθύρων, with Carrière.

47. This is a deliberate revision of some lines of Tyrtaeus.

48. This enigma has been thought to refer to a man (perhaps Solon) who had the power to make himself a tyrant, but refrained. The other interpretation – and I think the right one – is that the meaning is erotic – the speaker could have his way with the object of his admiration, but has not done so.

49. This poem is incomplete.

50. In other words, there would be no contest: with such a prize, the poet (mule) would easily beat his rival.

51. This is a slightly different version of a poem by Tyrtaeus.

52. This is by Mimnermus.

53. = ll. 853–4.

54. = ll. 877–8, one word different.

55. See ll. 213–18.

56. Slightly different version of ll. 39–42.

57. = ll. 87–90.

58. An incomplete poem.

59. = ll. 571–2.

60. = ll. 417.

61. cf. ll. 57–60.

62. = ll. 619–20, one word different.

63. Ploutos is the god of wealth.

64. Incomplete poem.

65. = ll. 1238a and b.

66. See ll. 1095–6.

67. = ll. 441–6.

68. See ll. 97–100.

69. = ll. 415–18.

70. = ll. 555–6.

71. = ll. 367–8.

72. In prose:

Son of Polypaös, I heard the shrill voice of the crying bird, which comes as a messenger to men, that it is the season for ploughing. It struck my black heart, because other men hold my blooming fields, nor do my mules pull the yoked plough, on account of the hateful sea-voyage.

(The text of this last line is doubtful. The poem is probably incomplete.)

73. Aethon was one of the pseudonyms used by Odysseus. The poem is still puzzling.
74. Lethe's plain: death.
75. This couplet and the three following are not in any manuscript but are quoted by other ancient authors.
76. Another riddle: the answer is a conch shell.
77. = ll. 1151-2.
78. = ll. 597.
79. Solon wrote this.
80. Text very uncertain.
81. = ll. 1101-2.
82. = ll. 949-50.
83. This phrase is mock epic: 'thou mightiest of boys'.
84. = ll. 1107-8.
85. This is probably by Euenos.
86. Poem incomplete.

SELECT GLOSSARY

Select Glossary

AEGIS: a magic cloth or shield, carried by Zeus or Athene. Perhaps it is a goatskin. If shaken, it puts panic into the hearts of men.

AIDONEUS: another name for Hades.

AMBROSIA: food of the gods. It apparently preserves their immortality.

APHRODITE: the great goddess of love. Also called Cytherea, Cyprogenes, Cypris, the Cyprian. Latin name: Venus.

APOLLO: often called Phoebus (shining) Apollo, he who shoots from far off. The archer god, patron of prophecy, music, medicine. Later associated with the sun.

ARES: the god of war, not admired by Homer or Hesiod. Husband or lover of Aphrodite. Latin name: Mars.

ARTEMIS: sister of Apollo, virgin goddess of wild animals and hunting; also, sometimes, of childbirth and fertility, and sudden, painless death. Latin name: Diana.

ATHENE: virgin goddess of crafts, of civilization, of cleverness. Personal patron of the hero Odysseus, and of the city of Athens. Latin name: Minerva.

ATLAS: Titan son of Iapetos who holds the sky up on his head and shoulders.

BOREAS: the north wind.

CYPRIAN, CYPROGENES, CYTHEREA: epithets of Aphrodite.

DEMETER: goddess of grain and the earth's fertility, mother of Persephone. Latin name: Ceres.

DIONYSUS: god of wine, dance, theatre, and uninhibited religious enthusiasm. Latin names: Bacchus, Liber.

EOS: the Dawn. Latin name: Aurora.

EPIMETHEUS: short-sighted brother of Prometheus. He started all the trouble for men by accepting Zeus's 'gift' of Pandora, the first woman.

EREBOS: 'the dark place', part of the underworld, or the underworld itself.

EROS: sexual love. In early Greek, an awesome, powerful force; later, more playful, equivalent to the Roman Cupid.

FURIES: Greek Erinues. Terrifying spirits of retribution, particularly interested in punishing crimes against the family.

GAIA, or GE: the goddess Earth. Her husband was Ouranos, Heaven, but she was quite capable of producing children without assistance from a male. In fact she produced Ouranos.

GORGONS: see Perseus.

HADES: a great god, brother of Zeus and king of the underworld. His wife is Persephone, whom he kidnapped from her mother Demeter. Latin names: Dis, Pluto.

HEBE: the goddess Youth, wife of the deified Heracles.

HELICON: the largest mountain in Boeotia, in Greece. Home of the Muses. Askra, where Hesiod lived, was on its slopes.

HELIOS: the sun.

HEPHAISTOS: the lame blacksmith god, patron of handcrafts, and one of the few Olympian gods who are consistently benevolent. Latin name: Vulcan.

HERA: the wife and sister of Zeus, queen of the Olympian gods. Patron of marriage and the family and the city of Argos, enemy of Heracles. Latin name: Juno.

HERACLES: a hero famous for his strength. He performed twelve celebrated labours and slew in the process many a monster. He was perhaps, originally, a real man, but by Hesiod's time had been deified. Latin name: Hercules.

HERMES: the gods' messenger, guide of souls to the underworld, patron of liars, thieves, and merchants. Latin name: Mercury.

IRIS: the rainbow, a swift messenger of the gods.

KRONOS: son of Ouranos and Gaia, father of Zeus. He castrated and dethroned his father, and was in turn overthrown by his son. He is often called 'clever' or 'crooked'.

LETO: the mother of Apollo and Artemis, by Zeus.

LIMPING GOD: Hephaistos.

MEDUSA: see Perseus.

MNEMOSYNE: Memory, the mother of the nine Muses.

MUSES: goddesses of song and poetry. Their individual functions had not yet been established in Hesiod's day.

NECTAR: drink of the gods.

NEMESIS: spirit of divine retribution.

NOTOS: the south wind.

OCEANUS: the river that encircles the earth. A prolific parent, he fathered the rivers and innumerable Oceanids (water nymphs).

OLYMPUS: a high mountain in Thessaly, where the gods were originally believed to live. By Hesiod's day, though, the name had become rather hazily connected with the sky, an equivalent to 'heaven'.

PANDORA: 'all gifts'. An artificial woman, sent to punish mankind for Prometheus' theft of fire.

PERSEPHONE: the queen of the underworld (see Hades) but also Demeter's daughter and a goddess of springtime and fertility. Latin name: Proserpina.

PERSES: Hesiod's no-good brother, to whom the *Works and Days* is addressed.

PERSEUS: a hero, the son of Zeus and Danae. He was sent by wicked king Polydektes to collect the head of Medusa the Gorgon. To look a Gorgon in the face would turn anyone to stone. With the help of Athene and Hermes, Perseus cut off the head and presented it to Polydektes, who was petrified.

PLOUTOS: the god of money.

POSEIDON: god of earthquakes, horses, and the sea. A powerful god, brother of Zeus. Latin name: Neptune.

PROMETHEUS: a god, friend and patron of mankind, who stole fire for men and taught them how to cheat the gods in sacrificing, and was punished by Zeus.

RHEA: the wife of Kronos, and mother of several important gods, including Zeus.

SELENE: the Moon.

TARTARUS: the lowest part of the underworld; or, the underworld itself.

TITANS: the children of Ouranos and Gaia, or any of the older race of gods who were challenged by the Olympians and defeated. They are now in Tartarus.

THEMIS: the personification of Law or Right, a goddess who married Zeus and bore the Hours and the Fates.

TYRSENIANS: Etruscans.

ZEPHYRUS: the gentle west wind.

ZEUS: the king of the Olympian gods, 'father of gods and men', bearer of the aegis, counsellor, thunderer, god of suppliants and guests, son of Kronos, husband and brother of Hera, lover of many, whose name probably means 'bright sky'. Latin name: Jupiter.